Edward Arber, John Penry, Martin Marprelate

The Epistle

September-November 1588

Edward Arber, John Penry, Martin Marprelate

The Epistle
September-November 1588

ISBN/EAN: 9783337728915

Printed in Europe, USA, Canada, Australia, Japan

Cover: Foto ©Lupo / pixelio.de

More available books at **www.hansebooks.com**

The English Scholar's Library of Old and Modern Works

MARTIN MARPRELATE

The Epistle

[September—November 1588]

EDITED BY

E D W A R D   A R B E R

F.S.A, ETC. LATE EXAMINER IN ENGLISH
LANGUAGE AND LITERATURE
TO THE UNIVERSITY OF
LONDON

WESTMINSTER

ARCHIBALD CONSTABLE AND CO.

1895

CONTENTS.

BIBLIOGRAPHY.

ISSUES IN THE AUTHORS' LIFETIME.

1 [Sept.–Nov. 1588. East Molesey, Surrey.] See *p.* 1.

ISSUES SINCE THEIR DEATH.

2. 1842. 71, Chancery Lane, London. 8vo. *Puritan Discipline Tracts.* The Epistle to the terrible Priests &c. [Edited by JOHN PETHERAM.] A second edition in 1843.

3. 2 August, 1880. Willesden, London, N.W. The present impression.

∴ *All as separate publications.*

I N T R O D U C T I O N.

 E HAVE seen in the *Introductory Sketch, &c.* (No. 8 of this Series), *pp.* 195, that this *Epistle* was the production of JOHN PENRY, assisted by JOB THROCKMORTON : and that they made use of some *memoranda* which Rev. JOHN UDALL, Preacher at Kingston, had made and which he had shewn in his study to the Vicar of that place, the Rev. STEPHEN CHATFIELD so far back as Michaelmas, 1587. *pp.* 83, 90, 171. But UDALL ever repudiated the mocking method of the presenting those facts which is adopted in the present Text. *p.* 118.

This *Epistle* was secretly printed in the "Dutch Letter," *p.* 114, by ROBERT WALDEGRAVE and JOHN PENRY in Mistress CRANE's country house at East Molesey in Surrey about Michaelmas, 1588 ; and came forth into furtive circulation from hand to hand, in the first days of the following November : previous to which date, neither the name nor the conception of MARTIN MARPRELATE (or as it was often, afterwards, for brevity's sake, reduced to, MARTIN) existed in English Literature.

Though PENRY alleged some previous similar works on the Continent (*Introductory Sketch, p.* 97) ; the character of "the reverend and worthie MARTIN MARPRELATE, gentleman," was quite an original one. On its surface, there was the coolest assurance in hobnobbing with their "venerable masterdomes"; the assumed testy merry wit, with the endless punning of DICK TARLETON ; all intermixed with the strongest possible home-thrusts and the most serious charges : while, beneath all this, there was the most earnest purpose of an outraged human nature, which considered it had found the Divine Messengers, in the most precious and sacred things of this mortal life, to be as " salt which had lost its savour "; and therefore only "fit to be cast out, and to be trodden under foot of men."

So the entire method of the Martinist issues is to try the Teachers of Religion at the bar of a Morality expressing simply the innate rights of Human Nature as such. And this was done with great daring ; and was, the times considered, utterly unexpected and strange : so that we cannot point to any attack on ELIZABETH's Privy Council for their secular trans- actions, comparable to that here made upon the members of her High Commission, for their ecclesiastical abuses.

Individual Bishops, like BONNER, had been reprehended before ; but, never, since AUGUSTINE the monk landed on the Isle of Thanet, had Bishops, *as a class*, been branded as "unlawful" or forbidden. So the *Demonstration* and the *Epistle* must have come on the Bishops like two bombshells ; and they, no doubt, occasioned inextinguishable merriment among the Puritan laity at the Court, and in the great cities of England.

Three times in modern English history, have the bulk of the clergy, as a class, been corrupt and rotten. In HENRY VIII.'s reign ; when the remedy came by the Reformation and the dissolution of the monasteries. In WHITGIFT's primacy ; when it came through the rise of the Puritans. In Queen ANNE's reign ; when it came through the lay-Reformers, the Moral Teachers, DEFOE, STEELE, and ADDISON, in their penny folio Half-Sheets, the *Review*, the *Tatler*, the *Spectator*, the *Guardian*, &c.

In 1588, a small minority of the Clergy, for the most part at work in towns, were intensely earnest, thoroughly pious and spiritually minded men : but with a narrowness of view, and no great learning, and conse- quently with little general culture. It was of their successors in the pulpit, the men who in the next generation became Scholars, that even their antagonist SELDEN said, about 1635, " All Confess there never was a more Learned Clergy, no Man taxes them with Ignorance " [*Table Talk*, s. v. *Clergy*]. But at this time, the Bishops were thrusting hundreds of men into the ministry of the Church, who were utterly unfit for their work.

With this active Clerical Remnant, went the best, the most cultured of the lay inhabitants of the towns, especially those near the South East seacoast. The Puritan Clergy and Laity together, were the Hope of the national life. In their long sufferance, integrity, prudence, and courage lay, potentially, all the possibilities of England. From them, we are.

On the other hand, their repression for a time, gave us our best Poetry and Drama ; which they would have thought it to be doing GOD service to have crushed : not recognizing the artistic faculty (the sense of form and beauty, colour and tone) to be an integral part of our nature ; and failing to acknowledge that fitness, suppleness, delicacy, subtlety, and finish are also among the blessed endowments of mankind. A rugged strength for right satisfied them, in the presence of so much wrong- doing.

II.

HE Martinist issues, and the similar rejoinders they provoked, are the chief Prose Satires of the Elizabethan Age. They approach to the nature of, but are not really lampoons ; such as may be seen in [ANDREW MARVELL's] *Advices to a Painter*, in SAMUEL BUTLER's *Posthumous Works*, and in DANIEL DEFOE's *Hymn to the Pillory*. A Lampoon is an attack on the private life of a man : but *MARTIN MARPRELATE* says, before his *Conditions of Peace*—

But you see my worshipfull priestes of this crue to whom I write / what a perilous fellow M. Marprelate is : he vnderstands of all your knauerie / and it may be he keepes a register of them : vnlesse you amend / they shall al come into the light one day. And you brethren bishops / take this warning from me. If you doe not leaue your persecuting of godly christians and good subiectes / that seeke to liue vprightly in the feare of God / and the obedience of her Maiestie / all your dealing shalbe made knowen vnto the world. And ise be sure to make you an example to all posterities. You see I haue taken some paynes with you alreadie / and I will owe you a better turne / and pay it you with aduauntage / at the least thirteene to the dozen / vnles you obserue these conditions of peace which I drawe betweene me and you. For I assure you I make not your doings known for anie mallice that I beare vnto you / but the hurt that you doe vnto Gods Churche / leaue you your wickednesse / and ile leaue the reuealing of your knaueries. *p.* 34.

and after them he adds—

These be the conditions / which you brethren bishops / shalbe bound to keepe inuiolably on your behalfe. And I your brother Martin on the other side / do faithfully promise vpon the performaunce of the premisses by you / neuer to make any more of your knauery knowne vnto the worlde. And howbeit that I haue before threatened my brother Bridges / in the cause of his superior priest / and your Antichristian callings : notwithstanding / I will write no more of your dealings / vnles you violate the former conditions. The conditions you see / are so reasonable / I might binde you to giue ouer your places which are Antichristian : but I doe not / lest men shoulde thinke me to quarrell / and seeke occasions for the nonce to fall out with my brethren. Therefore I require no more but such things as all the worlde will thinke you vnworthy to liue / if you grant them not. And this I doe the rather / because you should not / according to your olde fashion / say yat my worship doth for mallice lay open your infirmities: nay I haue published not one of your secret falts / what you haue not blushed to commit in the face of the sun / and in the iust[i]fiing wherof you yet stand / these things onely haue I published. The best seruants of God I know / haue their infirmities. But none of them will stand in the maintenance of their corruptions as you do / and that to the dishonour of God and the ruine of his Church. You must either amend / or shortly you will bring our church to ruine : therfore it is time that your dealings were better looked vnto. *p.* 36.

Thus *MARTIN* affirms his honesty of purpose and good intentions. But what extraordinary, and according to our present experience incredible things we find in this *Epistle*, may be gathered from *pp.* 7, 8.

III.

F THE nineteen Prelates named on those pages, most of them were born before the Reformation began in England with the arrival of TYNDALE's *New Testament* in 1526; and almost all of them were born before HENRY VIII.'s death. They were therefore brought up in Roman Catholic times.

On the other hand, PENRY, UDALL, and their colleagues, were for the most part, young men ; the children of the Elizabethan Age. So that the Martinist attack was the New School of young Radicals attacking the Old School of aged Conservatives. And this partly explains why there was no compromise sought out by the Bishops. They were too old to change : so they stood stiffly to their legal rights, and contemned anything like public opinion.

IV.

AD to relate. For the series of works, of which the *Epistle* was the first ; JOHN PENRY was hanged, suddenly for fear of tumult, on the 29th of May, 1593, not far short of five years after their first appearance : which act was the expression of the Bishops' sense of his share in their production.

V.

E GIVE on the next page a reproduction of the title page of Doctor BRIDGES's book, which was the groundwork of the whole attack; and to which *MARTIN MARPRELATE* refers when he says—

𝔒𝔥 read ouer 𝔇. 𝔍𝔬𝔥𝔫 𝔅ridges / for it is a worthy worke:

The *Defence* must have cost a great sum to print: for besides 8 *pp.* of *Preface to the Christian Reader*, it runs on, through Sixteen Books or Sections, to 1401 quarto pages of text. *MARTIN* maliciously says, at *p.* 11—

Nay I thinke you had more need to gather a beneuolence among the Cleargie / to pay Charde toward the printing of your booke / or els labour to his grace to get him another protection / for men wil giue no mony for your book / vnles it be to stop mustard pots.

It was one of the literary difficulties that these Puritan Free Lances had to overcome, to confute and overturn this big book without writing bulky books themselves. Hence the brief swift way in which each point is dealt with. Nothing like artistic form, or any general design running from one end of the book to the other, was attempted. The stories were inserted in any order, as they came to hand: but the attention of the reader never flags for an instant.

Special attention should be called to the noble exhortation at the end of the Epistle. How the Martinist books could ever be called "blasphemous," passes all comprehension.

A
DEFENCE OF THE
GOVERNMENT ESTABLISHED
IN THE CHVRCH OF ENGLANDE
FOR ECCLESIASTICALL MATTERS.

Contayning an aunswere vnto a Treatise called,
The Learned Discourse of Eccl. Gouernment,
otherwise intituled,

A briefe and plaine declaration concerning the desires of all the faithfull Ministers that haue, and do seeke for the discipline and reformation of the Church of Englande.

Comprehending likewise an aunswere to the arguments in a Treatise named
The iudgement of a most Reuerend and Learned man from beyond the Seas, &c.

Aunsvvering also to the argumentes of Caluine, Beza, and Danæus, with other our Reuerend learned Bretheren, besides Cænalis and Bodinus, both for the regiment of women, and in defence of her Maiestie, and of all other Christian Princes supreme Gouernment in Ecclesiasticall causes,

Against

The Tetrarchie that our Brethren would erect in euery particular congre-gation, *of Doctors, Pastors, Gouernors and Deacons, with their seuerall* and ioynt authoritie in Elections, Excommunications, Synodall Constitutions and other Ecclesiasticall matters.

Aunsvvered by *Iohn Bridges,* Deane of Sarum.

Come and See.
Joh. i. 36.

Take it vp and Read.
Aug. lib. conf. 8. *ca.* 12.

Printed by *Iohn Windet,* for *Thomas Chard.*
1 5 8 7

CONTROVERSIÆ PERSONÆ.

THE following were the chief Ecclesiastics against whom the present Text was written. In weighing the things laid to their charge, it must be remembered that many of them are only *ex parte* assertions ; and that some of them were afterwards wholly denied, or partially explained away.

ARCHBISHOP.

Oh read ouer D. John Bridges / for it is a worthy worke:

Or an epitome of the

fyrste Booke of that right worshipfull

volume / written against the Puritanes / in the defence
of the noble cleargie / by as worshipfull a prieste / John Bridges /
Presbyter / Priest or elder / doctor of Diuillitie / and Deane of
Sarum. Wherein the arguments of the puritans are
wisely preuented / that when they come to an=
swere M. Doctor / they must needes
say something that hath
bene spoken.

Compiled for the behoofe and overthrow

of the Parsons / Fyckers / and Currats / that haue lernt
their Catechismes / and are past grace: By the reuerend
and worthie Martin Marprelate gentleman / and
dedicated to the Confocationhouse.

The Epitome is not yet published / but it shall be when
the Byshops are at conuenient leysure to view the same.
In the meane time / let them be content with
this learned Epistle.

Printed oversea / in Europe / within two

furlongs of a Bounsing Priest / at the cost and
charges of M. Marprelate / gentleman.

❡ To the right puisante/and terrible

Priests/ my cleargie masters of the Confocation-
house/ whether fickers generall/ worshipfull Paltripo-
litans/ or any other of the holy league of subscription: this worke I
recommend vnto them with all my heart/ with a desire to see
them all so prouided for one day/ as I would wish/ which
I promise them shall not be at all to their hurt.

Ight poysond / persecuting and terrible priests /the theame of mine Epistle /vnto your venerable masterdomes / is of two parts (and the Epitome of our brother Bridges his booke / shall come out speedily) First / most pitifully complayning / Martin Marprelate / &c. Secondly / may it please your good worships / &c.

Most pitifully complayning therefore / you are to vnderstand / that D. Bridges hath written in your defence / a most senceles book / and I cannot very often at one breath come to a full point / when I read the same.

Againe / may it please you to giue me leaue to play the Duns for the nonce as well as he / otherwise dealing with master doctors booke / I cannot keepe *decorum personæ*. And may it please you / if I be too absurd in any place (either in this Epistle / or that Epitome) to ride to Sarum / and thanke his Deanship for it. Because I could not deal with his booke commendablie according to order / vnles I should be some-times tediously dunsticall and absurd. For I haue heard som cleargie men say / that M. Bridges was a verie patch and a duns / when he was in Cambridg. And some say / sauing your reuerence that are Bb. that he is as very a knaue / and enemy vnto the sinceritie of religion / as any popish pre-late in Rome. But the patche can doe the cause of sinceritie no hurt. Naye / he hath in this booke wonderfully graced

the same by writing against it.   For I haue hard some say /
that whosoeuer will read his booke / shall as euidently see
the goodnes of the cause of reformation / and the poore poore /
poore nakednes of your gouernment / as almost in reading all
master Cartwrights workes.   This was a very great ouersight
in his grace of Cant. to suffer such a booke to come out.
For besides that an Archb. is very weakely defended by masse
Deane / he hath also by this meanes prouoked many to write
against his gracious fatherhood / who perhaps neuer ment to
take pen in hand.   And brother Bridges / mark what martin
tels you / you will shortly I hope haue twenty fistes about
your eares more then your own.   Take heed of writing
against Puritanes while you liue / yet they say that his grace
woulde not haue the booke to be published / and if you marke /
you shall not finde seene and allowed in the title of the booke.
Well fare old mother experience yet / the burnt childe dreads
the fire : his grace will cary to his graue I warrant you / the
blowes which M. Cartwright gaue him in this cause : and
therefore no maruell though he was loth to haue any other so
banged as he himselfe was to his woe.   Others say that Iohn
Cant. ouersawe euery proofe.   If he did / then he ouersaw
many a foule salecisme / many a senceles period / and far more
slanders.   Slanders my friends ?   I thinke so.   For what
will you say / if our brother Bridges / and our cosen Cosins /
with manye others / haue had their grace of the Bb. *ad
practicandum* in Flanders ?   Howe could their gouernment
stand / vnles they should slander their brethren / and make her
Maiestie beleeue / that the Church gouerment prescribed in
the worde / would ouerthrow her regiment / if it were receiued
in our Church / and that the seekers of reformation / are a sort
of Malcontents / and enemies vnto the state.

    Item may it please your worthy worshipps / to receive this
curteously to fauour at my hand / without choller or laughing.
For my L. of Winchester is very chollericke and peeuish / so
are his betters at Lambeth / and D. Cosins hath a very good
grace in iesting / and I woulde he had a little more grace / and a
handful or two more of learning / against he answer the Abstract next.   Nay beleeue me / it is inough for him to answere
the Counterpoyson.   And I am none of the malicious sec-
taries / wherof Iohn of London spake the last Lent / 1588. in
his letters written to the Archdeacon of Essex / to forbid

publike fastes.   Ha / ha / D. Copcot are ye there / why do not
you answere the confutation of your sermon at Pauls crosse ?
It is a shame for your grace Iohn of Cant. that Cartwrights
bookes haue bene now a dozen yeares almost vnanswered :
you firste prouoked him to write / and you first haue receiued
the foyle.   If you can answer those books / why do you suffer
the puritans to insult and reioyce at your silence.   If you
cannot / why are you an Archb.   He hath prooued the calling
to be vnlawfull and Antichristian.   You dare not stand to the
defence of it.   Now most pitifully complayneth / M. Marprelate / desireth you either to aunswere what hath beene written
against the gracelesnes of your Archbishoprick / or to giue
ouer the same / and to be a meanes that no byshop in the land /
be a Lord any more.   I hope one day her Maiestie will either
see that the L. Bb. prooue their calling lawfull by the word /
or as Iohn of London prophesied saying / come downe you
bishopps from your thousands / and content you with your
hundreds / let your diet be pristlike / and not princelik / &c.
quoth Iohn Elmar in his Harborow of faithful subiects.   But
I pray you B. Iohn dissolue this one question to your brother
Martin : if this prophesie of yours come to passe in your
dayes / who shal be B. of London ? And will you not sweare
as commonly you do / like a lewd swag / and say / by my faith /
by my faith my masters / this geare goeth hard with vs.   Nowe
may it please your grace with ye rest of your worships / to
procure that the puritans may one day haue a free disputation
with you / about ye controuersies of the Church / and if you be
not set at a flat *non plus*, and quite ouerthrowen / ile be a Lord
B. my selfe : looke to your selues / I thinke you haue not long to
raigne.   Amen.   And take heed brethren of your reuerend and
learned brother Martin Marprelate.   For he meaneth in these
reasons following I can tell you / to proue that you ought not
to be maintained by the authoritie of the Magistrate / in any
Christian commonwealth : Martin is a shrewd fellow / and
reasoneth thus.   Those that are pettie popes and pettie Antichrists / ought not to be maintained in anie Christian commonwealth.   But euerie Lord B. in England / as for ilsample / Iohn
of Cant. Iohn of London / Iohn Excetor / Iohn Rochester /
Thomas of Winchester.   The B. of Lincolne / of Worcester / of
Peterborow / and to be briefe / all the Bb. in England /
wales / and Ireland / are pettie popes / and pettie Anti-

What mala-
pert knaues
are these that
cannot be con-
tent to stand
by and here/
but they must
teach a gentle-
man how to
speake.
christes.   Therefore no Lord B. (nowe I pray thee good Martin speake out / if euer thou diddest speake out / that hir Maiestie and the counsell may heare thee) is to be tollerated in any christian common welth : and therfore neither Iohn of Cant. Iohn of London / &c. are to be tollerated in any christian commonwelth.   What say you now brother Bridges / is it good writing against puritanes.   Can you denie any part of your learned brother Martin his syllogisme.   We denie your minor

Looke the
doctors booke/
pag. 107. line
20. and pag.
113. line 13.
M. Marprelat say the Bb. and their associats. Yea my learned masters / are you good at that ? what do you brethren ? say me that againe? do you denie my minor ?   And that be all you can say / to denie L. Bb. to be pettie popes / turne me loose to the priests in yat point/ for I am olde suersvie at the proofe of such matters / ile presently marre the fashion of their Lor[d]ships.

They are pettie popes / and pettie Antichrists / whosoeuer vsurpe the authority of pastors ouer them / who by the ordi- nance of God / are to bee vnder no pastors.   For none but Antichristian popes and popelings euer claimed this authoritie vnto themselues / especiallie when it was gainsaid / and ac- counted Antichristian / generally by the most Churches in the world.   But our L. bishops vsurpe authoritie ouer those / who by the ordinance of God / are to be vnder no pastors / and that in such an age / as wherein this authoritie is gainsaid / and accounted Antichristian / generally by all the Churches in the world for ye most part.   Therefore our L. Bb. what sayest thou man / our L. bishopps / (I say) as Iohn of Canterburie / Thomas of Winchester (I will spare Iohn of London for this time / for it may be he is at boules / and it is pitie to trouble my good brother / lest he should sweare too bad) my reuerend prelate of Litchfielde / with the rest of that

M. Marprelate
you put more
then the questi-
on in the con-
clusion of your
syllogisme.
swinishe rable / are pettie Antichrists / pettie popes / proud prelates / intolerable withstanders of reformation / enemies of the gospell / and most couetous wretched priests. This is a pretie matter/ yat standers by / must be so busie in other mens games : why sawceboxes must you be pratling ? you are as mannerly as bishops / in medling with that you haue nothing to doe / as they do in taking vpon them ciuill offices.   I thinke for any maners either they or you haue / that you were brought vp in

Bridewell.   But it is well that since you last interrupted me
(for now this is the second time) you seeme to haue lernt
your *Cato de moribus* in that you keepe your selues on the
margent.   Woulde you be answered ?   Then you must know /
that I haue set downe nothing but the trueth in the conclusion / and the syllogismes are mine owne / I may do what I
will with them / and thus holde you content.   But what say
you my horned masters of the Confocation house ?   you denie
my minor againe I know.   And thus I prooue it.   First

That our Prelates vsurpe their authoritie

They vsurpe their authoritie / who violently and vnlawfully /
retaine those vnder their gouernment / that both woulde and
ought (if they might) to shake of[f] that yoke wherewith they
are kept vnder.   But our Lord bishops retaine such (namely
other pastors) and vnlawfully vnder their yoke / who both
woulde and ought to reiect the same.   For all the pastors
in the land / that deserue the names of pastors / are against
their wil vnder the bishops iurisdictions.   And they are vnlawfully detained by them / because no pastor can be lawfully
kept vnder the pastoral (I meane not the ciuill) authoritie of
any one man.   Therfore our Bb. and proud popish / presump-
tuous / profane / paultrie / pestilent and pernicious prelates /
bishop of Hereforde and all : are first vsurpers to beginne the
matter withall.   Secondly

Our Prelates claime this authoritie ouer those / who by the ordinance of God / are to be vnder no Pastors.

That is / they claime pastorall authoritie ouer other ministers
and pastors / who by the ordinaunce of God / are appointed to
be pastors and shepheards to feede others / and not sheep / or
such as are to haue shepheards / by whom they are to be
fedd and ouerseene : whiche authoritie the bishops claime
vnto themselues.   For they say that they are pastors of
al the pastors within their dioces.   And take this of M.
Marprelates worde / that there is no pastor of pastors / but
he is a pope.   For who but a pope will claime this
authoritie.   Thirdly /

This authority of our L. Bb. in England, is accounted Antichristian of the most Churches in the worlde.

As of the Heluetian / the Scottish / French / Bohemian / and

the Churches of the low countries / the Churches of Polonia /
Denmarke / within the dominions of the Count Palatine / of
the Churches in Saxonie / and Sweuia / etc. which you shall
see euidently proued in the Harmonie of the Confessions of
all those Churches / Section the eleuenth. Which Harmonie /
was translated and printed by that puritan Cambridg printer /
Thomas Thomas. And although the booke came out by publike authoritie / yet by your leaue the Bishops haue called
them in / as things against their state. And trust me / his
grace will owe that puritane printer as good a turne / as hee
paid vnto Robert Walde-graue for his sawcines / in printing
my frend and deare brother Diotrephes his Dialogue. Well
frend Thomas I warne you before hand / look to your selfe.

And now brethren byshops / if you wil not beleeue me / I wil
set down the very words of the French confession / contayned
page 359. of the Harmonie. We beleeue (saith the confession / art 30.) that all true pastors / in what place soeuer they
be placed / haue the same / and equall authority among themselues / giuen vnto them vnder Iesus Christ the onely head /
and the chiefe alone vniuersal bishop: and that therefore it
is not lawfull for anye Churche to challenge vnto it selfe /
dominion or soueraignty ouer any other. What an horrible
heresie is this / wil some say / why? gentle Martin / is it possible yat these words of the French confession should be
true? is it possible that there ought to be an equallity
betweene his Grace and the Deane of Sarum / or som other
hedge priest : Martin saith it ought be so / why then Martin
if it shoulde be so / howe will the byshops satisfie the reader
in this poynt? Alas simple fellow whatsoeuer thou
art / I perceiue thou dost not mark the words of the
confession : My good brethren haue long since
taken order for this geare : For the Confession doth not say
that all Pastors / but that all true Pastors / and all Pastors
that are vnder Iesus Christ / are of equall authority. So that
all men see that my brethren / that are neyther true Pastors /
nor I feare me vnder Iesus Christ / ar not to be of equall
authority. And because this doth not touch them / I will
end this whole learned discourse with the words of Pope
Gregorie / vnto Iohn bishop of Constantinople (for I haue
red somthing in my dayes) which words you shall finde
in our owne Englishe Confession / written by a bish. page

At a dead lift well fare a good glose.

361. of the Harmony.   The Popes words be these / *He is also the king of pride, he is Lucifer, which preferreth* Put the case *himself before his brethren, he hath forsaken the fayth,* that my Lord *and is the forerunner of Antichriste.* And haue not of Canterbury is such a one. I quited my selfe like a man / and dealt very valiantly / in prouing that my lerned brethren the L. bishops ought not to be in any christian common wealth / because they are pettie Popes / and pettie Antichristes.   But what do you say / if by this lustie syllogisme of mine owne making / I proue them Popes once more for recreations sake.

Whosoeuer therefore clayme vnto themselues pastorall authoritie ouer those Christians / with whome they Why Martin / cannot possiblie at any time altogether in the same what meanest congregation sanctifie the Sabboth: they are thou? Certainely an vsurping prelats / Popes and pettie Antichrists: thou takest For did you euer here of anye but of Popes and that course dumb ministers / that would challenge the authority thou wilt set of Pastors ouer those Christians / vnto whom they thy good could not possiblie on the Sabboths discharge the brethren at their wits end. dutie of pastors: But our L. Bb. challenge vnto themselues pastorall authoritie ouer them / vnto whom they cannot possiblie on the Sabboth / discharge the duty of Pastors / vz. ouer people inhabiting diuers shires distant asunder / with whom / gathered together on the Saboth / they cannot by order of nature / performe any dutie of Pastors: Therefore all the L. Bishops in England / Ireland and Wales (and for the good wil I beare to the reuerende brethren / I will speake as loud as euer I can) All our L. Bb. I saye / are pettie Popes / and pettie vsurping Antichristes / and I thinke if they will still continue to be so / that they will breed yong Popes / and Antichristes: *per consequens,* neyther they nor their broode / are to be tollerated in any Christian common wealth / quoth Martin Marprelate.   There is my iudgment of you brethren / make ye most of it / I hope it will neuer be worth a byshopricke vnto you: reply when you dare / you shall naue as good as you bring.   And if you durst but dispute with my worship in these poynts / I doubt not but you should be sent home by weeping crosse.   I wold wish you my venerable masters for all that / to answere my resons / or out of doubt you will prooue pettie Antichristes / Your corner caps and tippets will do nothing in this poynt.

Most pitifully complayneth / Martin Marprelate / vnto your honorable masterships / that certayn theeues / hauing stolne from dyars in Thames streat / as much cloth as came to 30. pound / did hide the sayd cloth in Fulham / which is a place within the territories of the Lord dumbe Iohn / who by occupation is Lord Bish. of London : The theeues were apprehended / the cloth came within your clouches Don Iohn of London / and al is fish that comes to the net with your good Honor. The theeues being taken / the dyars came to challenge their cloth : Iohn London the bishop / sayd it was his owne / because it was taken within his owne Lordship. But sayth he / if the cloth be yours let the law go vpon the theeues / and then ile talke farther with you : wel / one or two of the theeues were executed and at their deathes confessed that to be the cloth which the bishop had / but the dyars coulde not get their cloth / nor cannot vnto this day / no though one of their honors wrote vnto him to restore the cloth vnto the poore men. What reason were it he should giue them their own / as though he could not tell how to put it vnto good vses as well as the right owners. It is very good blew / and so would serue well for the liueries of his men / and it was good greene / fit to make quishions and couerings for tables. Brother London / you were best to make restitution it is playne theft and horrible oppression : Bon[n]er would haue blusht / to haue bene taken with the like fact. The popish sort your brethren / will commend this vnto posteritie by writing assure your selfe. The dyars names are Baughin /

My booke shall come with a witnes before the high commission. Swan and Price : They dwell at the old swan in Thames streat / I warrant you Martin will be found no lyar / he bringeth in nothing without testimonie. And therefore I haue set downe the mens names and the places of their aboade / yat you of this conspiration house may finde out this slaunder of trueth / against the L. of good London. It was not therefore for nothing (Iohn of London I perceiue) that Mistris Lawson the shrew at Pauls gate / and enemie to all dumb dogs and tyrannicall Prelates in the land : bad you throw downe your selfe at hir Maiesties feet / acknowledging your selfe to be vnsauory salt / and to craue pardon of her highnes / because you had so long deceiued her and her people : You might well ynough craue pardon for your theft / for Martin wil stand to it / that the detayning of the mens cloth is plain theft.

Riddle me a riddle what is that / his grace threatened to
send Mistris Lawson to Bridewell / because she shewed the
good father D. Perne / a way how to get his name out of the
booke of Martyrs / where the turnecoat is canonized for burn-
ing Bucers bones: Dame Lawson aunswered / that she was
an honest Citizens wife / a man well knowen / and therefore
bad his Grace an he would / send his vncle Shorie thither.
Ha ha ha: Now good your grace you shall haue small
gaynes in medling with Margrete Lawson I can tell you.
For if she be cited before *Tarquinius Superbus* D. Stanop /
she will desire him to deale as fauorablie with her in that
cause / as he would with Mistris Blackwell / tse tse tse / wil
it neuer be better with you mistris Lawson.

Sohow / brother Bridges / when will you answere the booke
intituled / an answere to Bridges his slanders: nay I thinke
you had more need to gather a beneuolence among the
Cleargie / to pay Charde toward the printing of your booke /
or els labour to his grace to get him another protection / for
men wil giue no mony for your book / vnles it be to stop
mustard pots / as your brother Cosins answer to the Abstract
did. You haue bin a worthy writer as they say of a long
time / your first book was a proper Enterlude / called Gammar
Gurtons needle. But I thinke that this trifle / which sheweth
the author to haue had some witte and inuention in him /
was none of your doing: Because your bookes seeme to pro-
ceede from the braynes of a woodcocke / as hauing neyther
wit nor learning. Secondly / you haue to your mediocritie
written against the Papists: And since that time / you haue
written a sheete in rime / of all the names attributed vnto the
Lorde in the Bible / a worthy monument: what hath the hedge
priest my brother written anye more? O is / I crye him mercy /
he hath written this great volume which now I haue in hand
against his brethren. The qualities of this booke are many /
M.D. sheweth himselfe to be very skilfull in the learning of
ob and *Sol*, if euer you red olde Fa-Briccot vpon Aristotle:
M. Deanes manner of writing and his / are not much vnlike /
Doctor Terence of Oxforde and this Doctor / may be neere or
kindred for their learning. There bee periods in this learned
booke of great reason / though altogether without sence. I
will giue you a proof or two / page 441. *And although* (sayth
the Doctor) *Paule afterward,* 1 *Cor.* 1. 14, *mentioning this*

Crispus, term him not there, the archgouernour of the Iewes.
Sosthenes, and *Synagogue, yet as it farther appeareth, Acts* 18. 17. *by*
not Crispus *Sosthenes, who was long before a faythfull Christian,*
was one of the
72. Disciples. *and as some alledge out of Eusebius lib.* 1. *cap.* 13. *he*
was also one of the 72. *Disciples chosen by Christ,*

Fleering / iering / leering: there is at all no sence in this
period. For the words (yet afterward) vnto the ende / M.D.
minde was so set vpon a byshopricke / that he brought
nothing concerning Crispus to aunswere the word (yet)
Therefore I will helpe my reuerende brother to make the
sentence in this sort.   And although / &c. yet afterwarde my
learned brother / D. Yong / Bish. of Rochester / hauing the
presentation of a benefice in his hand / presented himselfe
thereunto / euen of meere goodwil.   I Iohn of Rochester /
present Iohn Young quoth the bishop.   Now iudge you good
readers / whether Martin sayth not true / that there is too
much consenage now a dayes among the cleargie men.

This sentence following of M. Deanes / hath as good sence
as the former / page 655.   The D. citeth these wordes out of
the learned Discourse.   *God graunt that in steede of ordinarye*
formes of prayers, wee may haue preaching in all places.   And in
steede of Amen / God forbidd saye I / quoth the Doctor / with
another prayer to the contrarye / now (nowe marke my
masters / whether you can finde anye sence in this contrarye
prayer / for I assure you reuerende Martin can finde none) *if*
These be the *it be his good will not so much (good lord) to punnish*
D. owne
words. *vs, that this our brethrens prayer should be graunted.*
If this be a senceles kinde of writing / I would there were
neuer a Lord bishop in England.

And lerned brother Bridges / a man might almost run himselfe
out of breath before he could come to a full point in many places
in your booke / page 69. line 3. speaking of the extraordinarye
giftes in the Apostles time / you haue this sweete learning.
Yea some of them haue for a great part of the time, continued euen
till our times, and yet continue, as the operation of great workes,
or if they meane miracles, which were not ordinary no not in that
extraordinary time, and as the hipocrites had them, so might and
had diuers of the papists, and yet their cause neuer the better, and the
who who/Dean *like may we say of the gift of speking with tongs which*
take thy breath *haue not bin with studie before learned, as Anthonie,*
and then to it
againe. *&c. and diuers also among the ancient fathers, and*

some among the papists, and some among vs, haue not bene desti-
tute of the giftes of prophesying, and much more may I saye this
of the gift of healing, for none of those giftes or graces giuen then
or since, or yet to men infer the grace of Gods election to be of
necessitie to saluation.

Here is a good matter deliuered in as good Gramaticall
words : But what say you if M. Do. can prooue that Peter
was prince of the Apostles ? That is popery (quoth Martin)
to begin withal. Nay but what say you if he pro-   Both these
ueth that one priest among the residue / may haue poynts are set
down page
a lawfull superiour authoritie ouer the vniuersall 448. line 3.
bodye of the Church / is not this plaine treason ? Is forsooth /
if a puritane had written it : But Mas Deane of Sarum that
wrote these things / is a man that fauoreth bishops / a non-re-
sident / one that will not sticke to play a game at Cards / and
sweare by his trothe : and therefore he may write against
the puritans what he will / his grace of Canterbury will giue
a verye Catholike exposition thereof.   This geare mayn-
teineth the crowne of Canterbury / and what matter is it
though hee write for the maintenaunce thereof / all the
treason in the world.   It wil neuer come vnto hir Maiesties
eare / as my friend Tertullus in the poore Dialogue that the
bishops lately burned hath set downe.   His grace is able to
salue the matter well inough : yea my brother Bridges himselfe can aunswere this poynt.   For hee hath written otherwise / page 288. line 26. in these wordes: *Neither is all*
gouernment taken away from all, though a moderate superior
gouernment be giuen of all to some, and not yet of all in all the
Churche to one, but to one ouer some in seuerall and particular
Churches.   The Deane wil say / that concerning the
superioritie of bishops this is the meaning. As concerning
the treason / written page 448. it may be the foxe D. Perne /
who helped him as they say / to make this worthy volume /
was the author of it.

Now brethren / if any of you that are of the Confocation
house / would knowe howe I can prooue M. Deane to haue
written flatt treason / page 448. as I haue before set downe :
draw neere / and with your patience I will proue it so / that
M. Deane will stand to his owne words / which I care not if
they be set downe : page 448. line 3.   Thus you shall read /
Doth S. Peter then forbid that any one Elder should haue and

exercise any superior gouernment ouer the cleargie, vnderstanding
I commend thee yet good D. for thy good English tongue.
the cleargie in this sence / *if he doth not but alloweth it, and his selfe practized it: then howsoeuer both the name, both of gouerning and cleargy may be abused, the matter is cleare, that one priest or elder among the residue, may haue*
Cleare quoth he / yea who wil make any question there- of.
a superior authority ouer the cleargie, that is, ouer all the vniuersall bodie of the church, in euery particular or seuerall congregation, and so not only ouer the people, but also ouer the whol[e] order of ministers.

Would your worships knowe howe I can shew and con-
uince my brother Bridges / to haue set downe flat treason in
the former words / Then haue at you Deane. 1. It is treason
Looke Stat. 13. Elizabeth.
to affirme her Maiestie to be an infidell or not to
be contayned in the bodie of the Church. 2 It is
treason to saye that one priest or elder / may haue a lawfull
superiour authoritie ouer hir Maiestie. Take your spectacles
then / and spell your owne words / and you shall finde that
you haue affirmed eyther of these 2. poynts. For you affirme
that a priest may haue a lawfull superior authoritie ouer the
vniuersall bodie of the Churche. And you dare not denie
her Maiestie to bee contayned within the vniversall bodie of
the Church. Therefore to helpe you to spell your conclusion /
you haue written treason / if you wil be as good as your
writing : your learned frend Martin (for no brother M. Deane
if you be a traytor) would not mistake you / and therefore say
what you can for your selfe : you meane not that this priest
shalbe ouer all the church : do you ? but howe shall we
knowe that ? forsooth because you saye that this superioritie
must be in euery particular or seuerall congregation. Is this
your aunswere brother Iohn ? why what sence is there in
these words ? One priest may haue a superior authoritie
ouer the vniuersal body of the Church / in euery particular or
seuerall congregation ? The vniuersal bodie of the Church /
is now become a particular or seuerall congregation with
you ? And in good earnest Deane Iohn / tell me howe many
orders of ministers be there in a particular congregation ?
For there must bee orders of ministers in the congregation /
where you meane this bounsing priest should haue his
superioritie / and because this cannot be in seuerall and particular congregations : therefore you cannot meane by these
words / ouer the vniuersall bodye of the Church / any other

thing / then the whole Church militant : But you would
mende your answere ? And say that this superior priest
must be an Englishe priest and no forrainer : As A good
for ilsample / his grace of Canterbury is an English ilsample.
priest. Do you meane then / that his grace should be this
superior priest / who by Sir Peters allowaunce may haue a
lawfull superior authoritie ouer the vniuersall Sir Peter
neuer alowed
bodie of the Churche ? Truely I doe not meane so. this.
And good now / do not abuse his graces worship in this sort /
by making him a Pope. Be it you meane this hie priest
should be no stranger / yet your treason is as great or greater.
For you will haue her Maiesty to be subiect vnto her owne
subiect and seruant. And if it be treason to say that the
Pope / who hath princes and Cardinalls for his seruants / being far better than were Iohn with his Canterburinesse / may
haue a lawfull superior authoritie ouer her Maiesty / as one
being contained with in the vniuersall bodie of the Church :
is it not much more trayterous to say / that an Englishe
vassall may haue this authoritie ouer his Soueraigne. And
brother Iohn / did Sir Peter his selfe in deede practize this
authoritie ? whie what a priest was he ? Did he Here be those
that can be
alow others to haue this authority. Truly this is barbarous as
well as masse
more then euer I knew til now. Yet notwith- Deane.
standing / I thinke he neuer wore corner cap and tippet in all
his life / nor yet euer subscribed to my Lord of Canterbury
his articles : Now the question is / whom Sir Peter his selfe
nowe alloweth to be this bounsing priest ? the Pope of Rome
yea or no ? No in no case / for that is against the statute.
For will my brother Bridges saye that the Pope may haue a
lawfull superior authoritie ouer his Grace of Canterbury ?
Ile neuer beleeue him though he saye so. Neyther will I
saye that his Grace is an Infidell / (nor yet sweare that he is
much better) and therefore M. Deane meaneth not that the
Pope shoulde bee this highe priest. No brother His grace
shall neuer get
Martin (quoth M. Deane) you say true / I meane me to sweare
against my
not that the Pope is this priest of Sir Peter. And conscience.
I haue many reasons why I shoulde denie him this authoritie. First he is a massemonger / that is / a professed
idolater. 2. He weareth a triple crowne / so doth not my
Lorde of Canterbury. 3 He hath his seat in Romish Baby-
lon in Rome within Italie : you know ye number 666. in the

Reuelation signifieth *Latenios*, that is / the man of Rome / or
Ecclesia Italike, the Italian church. Lastly / he must haue
men to kisse his toes / and must be carried upon mens
shulders / and must haue princes and kings to attend vpon
him / which sheweth his horrible pride. Sir Peters vniuersall priest and mine / shalbe no such priest I trow / ka Mas
Doctor. No shall not Doctor Iohn / I con thee thank. Then
thy vniuersall priest / 1. must be no idolator / 2. must be no
proude priest / and haue neuer a triple crowne (and yet I
hope he may weare as braue a sattin gowne as my Lord of
Winchester weareth / and he as cholericke as he) 3. he must
haue his seat out of Italie / as for fashion sake / at *Lambehith
Hippo / &c.* but at Rome in no case. If I should examine
these properties / I thinke some of them / if not all / haue bene
accidents vnto English priests. For how many Bb. are
there in England / which haue not either said masse / or
helped the priest to say masse or bene present at it ? As for
the triple crowne / Pope Ioan the English harlot hath woon
it : So did vrbane the 5. an English man. And concerning
pride / I hope that our Bb. nowe liuing / haue to their
mediocritie taken order / that some Popes may be inferior
vnto them / as for ilsample / his Canterburinesse / &c. And I
cannot see how the planting of the chaire in Rome any more
then Canterbury / can make a Pope. Seeing that Clement
the 5. Iohn 22. Benedict 12. and all other Popes / from the
yeare 1306. vnto 1375. sate not in Rome / but for the most
part at Avi[g]nion in Fraunce. But notwithstanding all this /
out of your meaning masse D. such a simple ingram man as
I am / in these poynts / of vniuersall superior priests / I finde
three differences betweene my L. of Peterborough / or any
other our high priests in England / and the Popes holines:
and 3. impediments to hinder the Pope from being Sir
Peters high priest and yours / vz. his idolatrie / 2. his triple
crowne / 3. his seat at Rome. But if Hildebrande Pope of
Rome / had beene a professor of the trueth (as his grace
Doctor turnecoats (Perne I shoulde saye) scholler is) had
worne no triple crowne / had bene Archbishop of Canterbury
(and I think we haue had Hildebrands there ere nowe) then
he might by the iudgement of the learned Bridges / and the
allowance of that Peter / which his selfe practized that
authoritie / haue a lawfull superior authority ouer the vni-

uersal bodie of the Church. And what a worthy Canterbury Pope had this bin / to be called my Lords grease? Thus
you see Brother Bridges / M. Marprelate an please him / is
able to make a yonger brother of you : he hath before proued /
that if euer you be Archb. of Canterbury (for you wrote this
foule heape against the holy Discipline of Christ / (as Whitgift
did the like) in hope to bee the next Pope of Lambeth)
that then you shalbe a pettie Pope / and a pettie Antichrist :
Nay he hath prooued you to haue deserued a cawdell of
Hempseed / and a playster of neckweed / asweel as some of
your brethren the papists. And now brother Bridges once
again / is it good writing against the Puritans. Take me at
my word / vnlesse you answere the former poynt of Anti-
christianisme / and this of treason / I will neuer write againe
to my bre[thren] the Bb. but as to vsurpers and Antichristes /
and I shall take you for no better then an enemie to her
Maiesties Supremacie. And because you haue taken vppon you
to defend L. Bb. though you be as very a sot as euer liued /
(outcept dumb Iohn of London againe) yet you shall answere
my reasons / or else I will so course you / as you were neuer
coursed since you were a Symonical Deane / you shall not
deale with my worshipp / as Iohn with his Canterburinesse
did with Thomas Cartwright / whiche Iohn / left the cause
you defend in the plaine field / and for shame threw downe
his weapons with a desperate purpose to runne away / and
leaue the cause / as he like a coward hath done : For this
dozen yeares we neuer saw any thing of his in printe for the
defence of his cause / and poore M. Cartwright doth content
himselfe with the victorie / which the other will not (though
in deed he hath by his silence) seeme to grant. But I will
not be this vsed at your hands / for vnlesse you answere me /
or confesse (and that in print) that al L. Bb. in Ha / priests ile
England / Wales / Ireland / yea and Scotlande to / bang you / or
                                                        els neuer trust
are pettie popes / and plaine vsurpers / and pettie me.
Antichristes : Ile kindle such a fire in the holes of these
foxes / as shall neuer be quenched as long as there is a L. B.
in England. And who but the worthie Martin can doe so
valiantly. Page 560. master Deane bringeth in Aretius / to
to proue that kneeling at the communion is not offensiue.
And how is the argument concluded thinke you ? forsooth
euen thus. Aretius saith / that in Berne they receiue the

communion sitting or standing : therefore saith my brother
Bridges / kneeling at the communion is not unlawfull.   I
maruell whether he was not hatched in a goose nest / that
would thus conclude.

In another place / page 226. or thereabouts / he prooueth
that one man may haue two spirituall liuings / because the puritans themselues saye / that one
charge may haue two ministers / to wit / a Pastor
and a Doctor.   And these be some of the good

*My brother
Bridges nowe
reasoneth in
good earnest
for nonresid-
ents.*

profes whereby our established gouernement is vphelde.

It would make a man laugh / to see how many trickes the
Doctor hath to coosen the sielie puritans in his book / he can
now and then without any noyse / alleadge an author clean against himselfe / and I warrant you /

*What a craftie
knaue is masse
Deane.*

wipe his mouth cleanly / and looke another way / as though
it had not bene he.   I haue laught as though I had bene
tickled / to see with what sleight he can throw in a popish
reason / and who sawe him ?   And with what art / he can
conuaye himselfe from the question / and goe to another
matter ? it is wonderfull to thinke.   And what would not a
Deane do to get a bishoppricke ?   In this one poynt / for
sparing labor he is to bee admired / that he hath set downe
vnder his owne name / those things which (to speak as I
think) he neuer wrote himselfe.   So let the puritans
aunswere when they will / he hath so much of other mens
helpes / and such contrarieties in this book / that when they
bring one thing against him out of his owne writings / he wil
bring another place out of the sayd booke / flat contrary to
that / and say that the latter is his / and not the former.   For
the former / it may bee / was some other friends / not so fullie
seene in the cause / as presbyter Iohn Bridges was.   The
reason of these contrarieties was very expedient : because
many had a hand in the worke / euery man wrote his own
minde / and masse doctor ioyned the whole together.

Nowe forasmuch as he hath playd the worthy workeman /
I will bestow an Epitaph vpon his graue when he dyeth /
which is thus :

Here lies Iohn Bridges, a worthie Presbyter he was.

But what if he be a B. before he die ? what brethren ? doe
you not thinke that I haue two strings to my bow / is vs haue
I / and thus I sing / if he chance to be a bishop.

Here lies Iohn Bridges late Bishop, friend to the Papa.

I care not an I now leaue masse Deanes worship / and be eloquent once in my dayes : yet brother Bridges / a worde or two more with you / ere we depart / I praye you where may a man buie such another gelding / and borow such another hundred poundes / as you bestowed vpon your good patron Sir Edward Horsey / for his good worde in helping you to your Deanry : go to / go to / I perceiue you will prooue a goose. Deale closeliar for shame the next time : must I needs come to the knoledge of these things ? What i, I should report abroad / that cleargie men come vnto their promotions by Simonie ? haue not you giuen me iuste cause ? I thinke Simonie be the bishops lacky. Tarleton tooke him not long since / in Don Iohn of Londons cellor.

Well nowe to mine eloquence / for I can doe it I tell you. Who made the porter of his gate a dumb minister ? Dumbe Iohn of London. Who abuseth her Maiesties subjects / in vrging them to subscribe contrary to lawe ? Iohn of London. Who abuseth the high commission / as much as any ? Iohn London / (and D. Stanop to) Whoe bound an Essex minister / in 200.l. to weare the surplice on Easter Ile make you weary of it dumbe Iohn / except you leaue persecuting. day last ? Iohn London. Who hath cut downe the Elmes at Fulham ? Iohn London. Who is a carnall defender of the breache of the Sabboth in all the places of his abode ? Iohn London. Who forbiddeth men to humble themselues in fasting and prayer before the Lorde / and then can say vnto the preachers / now you were best to tell the people / that we forbidd fastes ? Iohn London. Who goeth to bowles vpon the Sabboth ? Dumbe dunsticall Iohn of good London / hath done all this. I will for this time leaue this figure / and tell your venerable masterdomes a tale worth the hearing : I had it at the second hand : if he that tolde it me / added any thing / I do not commende him / but I forgiue him : The matter is this. A man dying in Fulham / made one of the bishopp of Londons men his executor. The man had bequeathed certaine Legacies vnto a poore shephearde in the towne. The shepheard could get nothing of the bishops man / and therefore made his mo[a]ne vnto a gentleman of Fulham / that belongeth to the court of requests. The gentlemans name is M. Madox. The poore mans case came to bee tryed in the court of Requestes.

The B. man desired his masters helpe : Dumb Iohn wrote to the Masters of requests to this effect / and I think these were his wordes.

My masters of the requests, the bearer hereof being my man, hath a cause before you : in as much as I vnderstande howe the matter standeth, I praye you let my man be discharged the court, and I will see an agreement made. Fare you well. The letter came to M. D. Dale / he answered it in this sort.

My Lorde of London, this man deliuered your letter, I pray you giue him his dinner on Christmas day for his labour, and fare you well.

Dumbe Iohn not speeding this way / sent for the sayd M. Madox : he came / some rough words passed on both sides / Presbyter Iohn sayde / master Madox was verye sawcie / especially seeing he knew before whom he spake : namely / the Lord of Fulham. Wherevnto the gentleman answered / that he had been a pore freeholder in Fulham / before Don Iohn came to be L. there / hoping also to be so / when he and all his brood (my Ladie his daughter and all) shoulde be gone. At the hearing of this speeche / the waspe got my brother by the nose / which mad him in his rage to affirme / that he woulde be L. of Fulham as long as he liued / in despight of all England. Naye softe there / quoth M. Madox / except her Maiestie I pray you / that is my meaning / ka dumb Iohn / and I tell thee Madox / that thou art but a Iacke to vse me so : master Madox replying / sayd that in deed his name was Iohn / and if euery Iohn were a Iacke / he was content to bee a Iacke (there he hit my L. ouer the thumbs) The B. growing in choller / sayd yat master Madox his name did shewe what he was / for sayth he / thy name is mad Oxe / which declareth thee to be an vnruly and mad beast. M. Madox answered againe / that the B. name / if it were descanted vpon / did most significantly shew his qualities. For said he / you are called Elmar / but you may be better called marelme / for you haue marred all the Elmes in Fulham : hauing cut them all downe. This farre is my worthy story / as worthye to bee printed / as any part of Deane Iohns booke / I am sure.

Item / may it please you that are L. Bb. to shewe your brother Martin / how you can escape the danger of a premunire / seeinge you vrge her Maiesties subiectes to subscribe / cleane contrary to the Statute. 13. Elizabeth. What haue

you to shew for your selues / for I tell you/I heard some say /
that for vrging subscription / you were all within the premunire /
insomuch that you haue bene driuen closely to buie your
pardons / you haue forfayted all that you haue vnto her
Maiestie / and your persons are voyde of her Maiesties
protection : you knowe the danger of a premunire I trowe ?
Well but tell me what you haue to shewe for your selues ? her
Maiesties prerogatiue ? haue you ?   Then I hope you haue it
vnder seale.   No I warrant you / her Maiesty is too wise for
that.   For it shall neuer be sayde / that she euer authorized
such vngodly proceedings / to the dishonor of God / and the
wounding of the consciences of her best subiects.   Seeing
you haue nothing to shew that it is her Maiesties will / why
should any man subscribe contrary to statute?   Forsoth men
must beleue such honest creatures as you are on your words?
must they ?   As though you would not lye : yes / yes / bishops
will lye like dogs.   They were neuer yet well beaten for
their lying.

May it please your honorable worships / to let worthy
Martin vnderstand / why your Canterburinesse and the rest of
the L. Bb. fauor papists and recusants / rather then puritans.
For if a puritane preacher / having a recusant in his parrish /
and shall go about to deale with the recusant for not
comming to Church.   Sir will the recusant say / you and I
will answere the matter before his grace / (or other the high
commissioners / as L. Bb. Seeuillaines (I meane) popish doctors
of the bawdie courts.)   And assoone as the matter is made
knowne vnto my Lorde / the preacher is sure to go by the
worst / and the recusant to carie all the honestie :   Yea the
preacher shalbe a busie enuious fellow / one that doth not
obserue the booke / and conforme himself according vnto
order / and perhaps go home by beggers bush / for any
benefice he hath to liue vpon. For it may be the Bb. will be so
good vnto him / as to depriue him for not subscribing.   As
for the recusant / he is known to be a man that must haue
the libertie of his conscience.   Is this good dealing brethren.
And is it good dealing / that poore men should be so troubled
to the chauncellors courte / that they are euen wearie of their
liues / for such horrible oppression as there raignes.   I tell
you D. Stannop (for all you are so proude) a premunire will
take you by the backe one day / for oppressing and tyranniz-
ing ouer her Maiesties subiects as you doe.

Doth your grace remember / what the Iesuit at Newgate sayde of you / namely / that my Lorde of Canterbury should surely be a Cardinall / if euer poperie did come againe into England : (yea and that a braue Cardinall to) what a knaue was this Iesuit? beleeue me I would not say thus much of my Lord of Canterburie / for a thousand pound / lest a *Scandalum magnatum* should be had against me : But well fare him that sayd thought is free.

Pitifully complayning / is there any reason (my Lords grace) why knaue Thackwell the printer / which printed popishe and trayterous welshe bookes in wales / shoulde haue more fauour at your gracelesse handes / then poore Walde-graue / who neuer printed book against you / that contayneth eyther treason or impietie. Thackwell is at libertie to walke where he will / and permitted to make the most he could of his presse and letters : whereas Robert Walde-graue dares not shew his face for the bloodthirstie desire you haue for his life / onely for printing of bookes which toucheth the bishops Myters. You know that Walde-graues printing presse and Letters were takken away : his presse being timber / was sawen and hewed in pieces / the yron work battered and made vnseruiceable / his Letters melted / with cases and other tooles defaced (by Iohn Woolfe / alias Machiuill / Beadle of the Stationers / and most tormenting executioner of Walde-graues goods) and he himselfe vtterly depriued for euer [of] printing againe / hauing a wife and sixe small children. Will this monstrous crueltie neuer bee reuenged thinke you? When Walde-graues goods was to be spoiled and defaced / there were some printers / that rather then all the goods should be spoyled / offered money for it / towardes the reliefe of the mans wife and children / but this coulde not be obtayned / and yet popishe Thackwell / though hee printed popish and trayterous bookes / may haue the fauor to make money of his presse and letters. And reason to[o]. For Walde-graues profession ouerthroweth the popedome of Lambehith / but Thackwels popery maintayneth the same. And now that Walde-graue hath neither presse nor letters / his grace may dine and sup the quieter. But looke to it brother Canterburie / certainly without your repentance / I feare me / you shalbe *Hildebrand in deed. Walde-graue hath left house and home / by reason of your

A fyrebrand in deede.

vnnaturall tyrannie : hauing left behinde him a poore wife and sixe Orphanes / without any thing to relieue them. (For the husband you haue bereaued both of his trade and goods) Be you assured that the crie of these will one day preuaile against you / vnlesse you desist from persecuting. And good your grace / I do now remember my selfe of another *More knauery printer /* that had presse and letter in a place called Charterhouse in London (in Anno 1587. neere about the time of the Scottish Queenes death) inteligence was giuen vnto your good grace of the same / by some of the Stacioners of London / it was made knowen vnto you what worke was in hand / what letter the booke was on / what volume / vz. in 8[v]o. in halfe sheetes / what workemen wroght on the same : namely / I.C. the Earle of Arundels man and three of his seruants / with their seuerall names / what liberallitie was bestowed on those workemen / and by whom / &c. Your grace gaue the Stationers the hearing of this matter / but to this daye the parties were neuer calde in Coram for it : but yet by your leaue my Lord / vpon this information vnto your honorable worship / the stacioners had newes / that it was *Is not he a very Pope in* made knowne vnto the printers / what was done *deed that thus hideth poperie* vnto your good grace / and presently in steed of the *and knauery.* work which was in hand / there was other appointed / as they saye / authorized by your Lordship. I will not saye it was your owne doing / but by your sleeue / thought is *It may be you* free. And my good L. (nay you shalbe none of my *hindred her Maiestie of* L. but M. Whitgift and you will) are you partiall *many thousands of* or no in all your actions tell me ? yes your are ? I *pounds.* will stand to it ? did you get a decree in the high court of Starchamber onely for Walde-graue ? if it bee in generall (and you not partiall) why fet you not that printing presse and letters out of Charterhouse / and destroye them as you did Walde-graues ? Why did you not apprehend the parties / why ? Because it was poperie at the least / that was printed in Charterhouse : and that maintayneth the crowne of Canterburye ? And what is more tollerable then popery ? Did not your grace of late erecte a new printer contrary to the foresayd decree ? One Thomas Orwine (who sometimes wrought popish bookes in corners : namely Iesus Psalter / our Ladies Psalter / &c.) with condition he should print no such seditious bookes as Walde-graue hath done ? Why my

This is no knauery my Lord. Lorde?   Walde-graue neuer printed any thing against the state / but onely against the vsurped state of your Paultripolitanship / and your pope holy brethren / the Lorde B. and your Antichristian swinish rable / being in-tollerable withstanders of reformation / enemies of the Gospell / and most couetous wretched / and popish priests.

Nowe most pitifully complayning / Martin Marprelate : That the papistes will needs make vs beleeue / that our good Iohn of Canterbury and they / are at no great iarre in religion. For Reignolds the papist at Rheimes / in his booke against M. Whitakers / commendeth the works written by his grace / for the defence of the corruption in our Churche / against T. Cartwright.   And sayth that the said Iohn Cant. hath many things in him / which euidently shew a catholike per-swasion.   Alas my masters shall we loose our metropolitan in this sort.   Yet the note is a good note / that we may take heed the Spaniards steale him not away / it were not amisse if her Maiestie knew of it.   Wee need not fear (if we can keep him) the Spaniards and our other popish enemies / because our metropolitans religion and theirs differ not much. In the article of Christes descending into hell / they iumpe in one right pat : and in the mayntenaunce of the hierarchie of Bb. and ascribing the name of priest / vnto them that are ministers of the gospel.   I know not whether my next tale will be acceptable vnto his grace or not.   But haue it among you my masters : M. Wiggington the pastor of Sidborough / is a man not altogether vnknowen vnto you.   And I think his worshipfull grace got little or nothing by medling with him / although he hath depriued him.   My tale is of his depriuation / which was after this sort. The good quiet people of Sydborough / being troubled for certaine yeares with the sayde Wiggington / and many of them being infected by him with the true knowledge of the gospell / by the worde preached (which is an heresie / that his grace doth mortally abhorre and persecute) at length grew in disliking with their pastor / because the seuere man did vrge nothing but obedi-ence vnto the gospell.   Well / they came to his grace to finde a remedie hereof : desiring him that Wiggington might be depriued.   His grace could find no law to depriue him / no although the pastor defied the Archb. to his face / and would giue him no better title then Iohn Whitgift / such buggs words / being in these daies accounted no lesse then high treason against a Paltripolitan : Though since that time / I think his grace hath bin well enured to beare the name of Pope of Lambeth / Iohn Cant. the prelate of Lambeth / with diuers other titles agreeable to his function. Well Sidborogh men proceeded against their pastor / his grace woulde not depriue him / because he could finde no law to warrant him therein / and he will do little contrary to law / for fear of a premunire / vnles it be at a dead lift / to depriue a puritan preacher. Then in deed he will do against lawe / against God / and against his owne conscience / rather then that heresie of preaching should preuail. One man of Sidborough / whose name is Atkinson / was very eger among the rest / to haue his pastor depriued : and because his grace woulde not heare them but departed away / this Atkinson desired his grace to resolue him and his neighbours of one poynt which something troubled them : and that was / whether his grace or Wiggington were of the deuil. For quoth he / you are so contrary the one from the other / that both of you cannot possibly be of God. If he be of God / it is certaine you are of the deuill / and so cannot long stand : for he will be your ouerthrowe. Amen. If you are of God / then he is of the duell as wee thinke him to be / and so he being of the deuill / will not you depriue him ? why shoulde you suffer such a one to trouble the Church. Now if he be of God / why is your course so contrary to his? and rather / why do not you follow him / that we may do so to ? Truely / if you do not depriue him / we will thinke him to be of God / and go home with him / with gentler good will towardes him / then we came hyther with hatred / and looke you for a fall. His grace hearing this northen logicke / was mooued on the sodaine youmust thinke / promised to depriue Wiggington / and so he did. This Atkinson this winter 1587 [*i.e.* 1587-8]. came vp to London / being as it seemed afflicted in conscience for this fact / desired Wiggington to pardone him and offred to kneele before her Maiestie / that Wiggington might bee restored againe to his place / and to stande to the trueth hereof / to his graces teeth. The man is yet aliue / he may be sent for / if you thinke that M. Martin hath reported an untrueth. No I warrant you / you shall not take mee to haue fraught my booke with lyes and slaunders / as Iohn Whitgift / and the Deane of Sarum did theirs. I speak not of things by heresay as of reports / but I bring my witnesses to prooue my matters.

May it please you to yeeld vnto a suite that I haue to your worships. I pray you send Wiggington home vnto his charge againe / I can tell you it was a foule ouersight in his grace / to send for him out of the North to London / that he might outface him at his owne doore. He woulde do his Canterburines lesse hurt if he were at his charge / then now he doth. Let the Templars haue M. Trauers their preacher restored againe vnto them / hee is now at leysure to worke your priesthood a woe I hope. If suche another booke as the Ecclesiast. Discipline was / drop[t] out of his budget / it were as good for the Bb. to lie a day and a night in little ease in the Counter. He is an od fellowe in folowing an argument / and you know he hath a smooth tong / either in Latine or English. And if my L. of Winchester vnderstood / eyther greeke or Hebrew / as they say he hath no great skill in neyther : I woulde praye your priestdomes to tell me which is the better scholler / Walter Trauers / or Thomas Cooper. Will you not send M. Wyborne to Northampton / that he may see some fruits of the seed he sowed there 16. or 18. yeares ago. That old man Wiborne / hath more good learning in him / and more fit gifts for the ministery in his little toe / then many braces of our Lord Bb. Restore him to preaching againe for shame. M. Paget shalbe welcome to Deuonshire / he is more fit to teach men then boyes. I marueile with what face a man that had done so much good in the Churche as he did among a rude people / could be depriued.

Except persecuting Greenefielde.

Briefely / may it please you to let the Gospell haue a free course / and restore vnto their former libertie in preaching / all the preachers that you haue put to silence : and this far is my first suit.

My 2. suit is a most earnest request vnto you / that are the hinderers of the publishing of the confutation of the Rhemish Testament by M. Cartwright / [that it] may be published. A resonable request / the granting whereof / I dare assure you / would be most acceptable vnto all that feare God / and newes of wofull sequell vnto the papists. For shall I tell you what I heard once / from the mouth of a man of great learning and deepe iudgement / who saw some part of Master Cartwrights answere to the sayde Rhemish and trayterous Raffodie ? His iudgment was this. That M. Cartwright had dealt so soundly against the papists / that for the answering and confuting of the aduersary / that one worke woulde be sufficient alone. He farther added / that ye aduersary was confuted by strange and vnknown reasons / that would set them at their wits end / when they see themselues assayled with such weapons / whereof they neuer once drempt / that they should be stroken at. And wil your grace or any els / that are the hinderers of the publishing of this worke / still bereaue the Church of so worthie a Iewell: nay / so strong an armour against the enemie. If you deny me this request / I will not threaten you / but my brother Bridges / and Iohn Whitgiftes bookes shall smoke for this geare / ile haue my peniworths of them for it.

Now may it please you to examine my worthines your brother Martin / and see whether I saide not true in the storie of Gyles Wiggington / where I haue set down / yat the preaching of the word is an heresie which his grace doth mortally abhorre and persecute / I can prooue it without doubt. And first that he persecuteth the preaching of the worde (whether it be an heresie or not) both in the preacher and the hearer: the articles of subscription / the silencing of so many learned and worthy preachers do euidently shew / and if you doubt hereof / let my worshipp vnderstand thereof / and in my next treatize / I shal prooue the matter to be cleare with a witnes / and I hope to your smal commendations / that will deny such a cleare point. On the other side / that he accounteth preaching to be an heresie / I am now to insist on the proofe of that poynt. But first you must know / that he did not account simple preaching to be an heresie / but to holde that preaching is the onely ordinary meanes to saluation / this he accounteth as an heresie / this he mortally condemned. The case thus stoode / Iohn Penrie the welsheman (I thinke his grace and my brother London / would be better acquainted with him and they could tell howe) about the beginning of Lent / 1587 [*i.e.* 20th February 1588]. offered a supplication and a booke to the Parliament / entreating that some order might be taken / for calling his countrie vnto the knowledge of God. For his bolde attempt / he was called before his grace with others of the high commission / as Thomas of Winchester / Iohn London / &c. After that his grace had eased his stomacke in calling him boy/knaue/ varlet/slanderer / libeller / lewde boy / lewd slaunderer / &c. (this is true/for I haue seene the notes of their conference/ at the length a poynt of his booke began to be examined) where nonresidents are thought intollerable. Here the Lorde of good London asked M. Penrie/what he could say against that kinde of cattell / aunswere was made that they were odious in the sight of God and man/because as much as in them lie/they bereaue the people ouer whom they thrust themselues/of the ordinarie meanes of saluation/which was the word preached. Iohn London demaunded whether preaching was the onely meanes to saluation? Penrie answered/that it was the onely ordinarie meanes/although the Lorde was not so tyed vnto it / but that hee could extraordinarily vse other meanes. That preaching was the onely ordinary meanes/he confirmed it by those places of scripture/ Rom. 10. 14. 1. Cor. 1. 21. Ephes. 1. 13 This point being a long time canuassed / at the length his worship of Winchester rose up / and mildly after his maner/brast forth into these words. I assure you my Lords/it is an execrable heresie: An heresie (quoth Iohn Penry) I thanke God that euer I knewe that heresie : It is such an heresie/that I will by the grace of God/sooner leaue my life then I will leaue it. What sir/(quoth the Archb.) I tell thee it is an heresie/and thou shalt recant it as an heresie? Naye (quoth Penrie) neuer so long as I liue godwilling. I will leaue this storie for shame/ I am weary to hear your grace so absurd. What say you to this geare my masters of the confocation house? we shal haue shortly a good religion in England among the bishops? if Paule be sayd of them to write an heresie. I haue hard some say/that his grace will speake against his own conscience? It is true. The proofe whereof / shalbe his dealing with another welshman/one M. Euans. An honorable personage/ Ambrose Dudley/nowe Earle of Warwicke (and long may he be so/to the glorie of God/the good of his Church/and the comfort of all his) in the singular loue he bare to the town of Warwick/would haue placed M. Euans there. To the ende that master Euans might be receiued with a fauorable subscription / &c. he offered the subscription which the Stat[ute]. requireth (wherevnto men may subscribe with a good conscience) The earl sent him with his letter / to his grace-lesnes of Cant. thinking to obtaine so smal a curtesy at his

hands. And I am sure / if he be Ambrose Dudley / the noble
Earle of Warwicke (whose famous exploytes / both in peace
and war / this whole land hath cause to remember with
thankfulnes) yat he is able to requite your kindnes / M. Iohn
Cant. O said his grace to M. Euans / I knowe you to be
worthy a better place then Warwicke is / and I would very
gladly gratifie my Lord / but surely / there is a Lord o Monstrous
in heuen whom I feare / and therefore I cannot hypocrite.
admit you without subscription. Thus the man with his
poore patrone / the earle of Warwick / were reiected by your
grace / and the poore earle to this day / knoweth not how to
finde the fauour at your hands / that the man may be placed
there. I tell you true Iohn Canter. If I were a noble man /
and a Counsellor to[o] / I should be sicke of the splene : nay I
could not beare this at your hands / to be vsed of a priest
thus / contrary to the law of God and this land. It is no
maruell though his honor could not obtaine this small suit
at your graceles hands / for I haue hearde your owne men
say / that you will not be beholding to neuer a noble man in
this land / for you were the 2. person / &c. Nay your own
selfe spake proudly / yea and that like a pope : when as a
worthy knight was a suter vnto your holines / for one of
Gods deare children (whom you haue kept and do keepe in
prison) for his libertie. You answered him he should lie
there stil / vnless he would put in sureties vpon such bonds
as neuer the like were hard of : and said further / that you
are the 2. person in the land / and neuer a noble man / nor
Counsellor in this lande should release him : Onely her
Maiestie may release him / and that you were sure / shee
would not. Doe you thinke this to be he (I pray you) that
was somtime doctor Pernes boy / and carried his cloakbagg
after him ? Beleeue me he hath leapt lustily ? And do not
you knowe that after it is full sea / there followeth Is not this
ambitious
anie b[b] ? Remember your brother Haman ? Do wretche at the
highest thiuke
you think there is neuer a Mordecai to step to our you.
Gracious Hester / for preseruing the liues of her faithfullest
and best subiects / whom you so mortally hate / and bitterly
persecute ? I hope you haue not long to raigne. Amen. And
you M. bishop of Worcester / how delt you with master
Evans in the same case ? Do you thinke that I do not
know your knauerye ? you could by lawe require no other

subscription of master Evans then he offered / and yet forsoth you would not receiue it at his handes / vnlesse he woulde also enter into a bonde / to obserue the booke of common prayer in euerie poynt / will law permit you to play the tyrant in this sort bishop ?   I shall see the premunire on the bones of you one day for these pranks.   And the masmonger your neighbor the B. of Glocester / thinks to go free / because in his sermon at Paules crosse / preached 1586. / in the Parliament time / he affirmed / that beefe and brewesse had made him a papist.   But this will not serue his turne : woulde you know what he did ? why he conuented an honest draper of Glocester / one Singleton / and vrged him being a lay man to subscribe vnto the booke.   The man affirming that no such thing cold be required of him by law / denied to subscribe : Vpon his deniall the B. sent him to prison.   Is it euen so / you old popish priest ? dare you imprison lay men for not subscribing ?   It were not good for your corner cap that her maiestie knew her subiects to be thus delt with. And if this be euer made knowen vnto her / I hope to see you in for a bird.   But brother Winchester / you of al other men are most wretched / for you openly in the audience of many hundreds / at sir Marie Oueries church the last lent / 1587. pronounced that men might finde fault / if they were disposed to quarrell / as well with the Scripture / as with the booke of Common praier.   Who coulde heare this comparison without trembling.   But lest you should thinke that he hath not as good a gift in speaking against his conscience / as my L. of Cant. is endued with : you are to vnderstand / that both in that sermon of his / and in another which he preached at the court the same Lent / he protested before God / and the congregation where he stood / yat there was not in the world at this day : nay there had not bin since the Apostles time / such a flourishing estate of a Church / as we haue now in England.   Is it any maruaile that we haue so many swine / dumbe dogs / nonresidents with their iourneimen the hedge priests / so many lewd liuers / as theeues / murtherers / adulterers / drunkards / cormorants / raschals / so many ignorant and atheistical dolts / so many couetous popish Bb. in our ministery : and so many and so monstrous corruptions in our Church / and yet likely to haue no redresse : Seing our impudent / shamelesse / and wainscote

O blasphemous wretche.

A flattering hypocrit.

faced bishops / like beasts / contrary to the knowledge of all
men / and against their own consciences / dare in the eares of
her Maiestie / affirme all to be well / where there is nothing
but sores and blisters / yea where the grief is euen deadly at
the heart. Nay saies my L. of winchester (like a monstrous
hypocrite / for he is a very duns / not able to defende an argument / but till he come to the pinch / he will cog and face it
out / for his face is made of seasoned wainscot / and wil lie as
fast as a dog can trot) I haue said it / I doe say it / and I haue
said it. And say I / you shall one day answere it (without
repentance) for abusing the Church of God and her Maiestie
in this sort. I would wish you to leaue this villanie / and the
rest of your diuellishe practises against God his saintes / lest
you answere it where your pieuish and chollerick simplicitie
will not excuse you. I am ashamed to think that the Churche
of England shoulde haue these wretches for the eyes thereof /
that woulde haue the people content themselues with bare
reading onely / and holde that they may be saued thereby
ordinarily. But this is true of our Bb. and they are afraid
that any thing should be published abrod / whereby the
common people should learne / that the only way to saluation /
is by the word preached. There was the last sommer a little
catechisme / made by M. Dauison and printed by Walde-
graue : but before he coulde print it / it must be authorized
by the Bb. either Cante. or London / he went to Cant. to
haue it licensed / his grace committed it to doctor Neuerbe-
good (Wood) he read it ouer in halfe a yeare / the booke is a
great one of two sheets of paper. In one place of the booke
the meanes of saluation was attributed to the worde preached :
and what did he thinke you ? he blotted out the word
(preached) and would not haue that word printed / so
ascribing the way to work mens saluation to the worde read.
Thus they doe to suppresse the trueth / and to keep men in
ignorance. Iohn Cant. was the first father of this horrible error
in our Church / for he hath defended it in print / and now as
you haue hard / accounteth the contrary to be heresie. And
popish Good / man / Abbot of Westminster / preaching vpon 12.
Rom. 1. said / that so much preaching as in some places we
haue is an vnreasonable seruice of God. Scribes / Pharises
and hypocrits / that will neither enter in [y]our selues / nor
suffer those that will / to enter heauen.

May it please your Priestdomes to vnderstand / that doctor
Cottington Archdeacon of Surrey / being belike bankerout in
his owne countrie / commeth to Kingstone vpon Thames of
meere good will that he beareth to the towne (I should say /
to vserer Haruies good chear and money bags) being out at
the heeles with all other vserers / and knowing him to be a
professed aduersary to M. Vdall / (a notable preacher of the
Gospell / and vehement reprouer of sinne) taketh the aduantage of their controuersie / and hoping to borow some of the
vserers money : setteth himself most vehemently against M.
Vdall / to do whatsoeuer Haruie the vserer will haue him :
and taketh the helpe of his iourniman doctor Hone / the
veriest coxcombe that euer wore veluet cap / and an ancient
foe to M. Vdall / because (in deed) he is [a] popish dolt / and (to
make vp a messe) Steuen Chatfield / the vicker of kingston /
as very a bankerout and duns as Doc. Cottington (although he
haue consumed all the money he gathered to build a Colledge
at Kingstone) must come and be resident there / that M.
Vdall may haue his mouth stopped / and why ? forsoth because
your friend M. Haruie woulde haue it so : for sayth Haruie /
he rayleth in his sermons / is that true ?   Doth he rail / when
he reproueth thee (and such notorious varlets as thou art) for
thy vsery / for thy oppressing of the poore / for buying the
houses ouer their heads that loue the gospell / and the Lord
his faythfull minister? (M. Vdall)   And art not thou a
mo[n]strous atheist / a belly God / a carnall wicked wretch /
and what not. M. Chatfield you thinke I see not your knauery?
is vs do I / you cannot daunce so cunningly in a net but I can
spie you out ? shal I tel you why you sow pillowes vnder
Haruies elbowes ? Why man / it is because you would borow
an 100. pound of him ? Go to you Asse / and take in M.
Vdall againe (for Haruie I can tell / is as craftie a knaue as
you / he will not lend his money to such bankerouts / as Duns
Cottington and you are) and you do not restore M. Vdall
againe to preach / I will so lay open your vilenes / yat I wil
make the very stoones in Kingstone streets shall smell of your
knaueries. Nowe if a man aske M. Cottington why M. Vdall
is put to silence ? forsoth saith he / for not fauoring the
Churche gouernement present.   Doc. Hone (Cottingtons
iourniman / a popish D. of the baudy court) saith by his troth /
for making such variance in the town. M. Chatfield seemeth

to [be] sorie for it / &c. But what cause was alleaged why M.
Vdall must preach no longer ? surely this onely? that he
had not my L. of Winchesters licence vnder seale to shew :
and because this was thought not to be sufficient to satisfie
the people : Hone the baudie Doctor / charged him to be a
sectarie / a schismatike / yea he affirmed plainly / that the
gospell out of his mouth was blasphemie. Popish Hone / do
you say so ? do ye ? you are a knaue I tel you ? by ye same
token your friend Chatfield spent thirteene score pounds in
distributing briefes / for a gathering towards the erecting of a
Colledge at kingstone vpon Thames.

Wohohow / brother London / do you remember Thomas
Allen and Richard Alworth / marchants of London / being
executors to George Allen somtimes your grocer / but now
deceased : who came vnto you on easter wednesday last being
at your masterdoms pallace in London / hauing bene often to
speake with you before and could not / yet now they met with
you : who tolde you they were executors vnto one George
Allen (somtimes) your grocer / and among other his debts / we
finde you indebted vnto him / in the some of 19. pound and
vpward / desiring you to let them haue the money / for that
they were to dispose of it according to that trust he reposed
in them. You answered them sweetly (after you Can B. face,
had pawsed a while) in this maner: You are cog lie and
raskals / you are villaines / you are arraunt knaues / I thinke you.
owe you nought / I haue a generall quittance to shew. Sir
(sayd they) shew vs your discharge / and wee are satisfied.
No (quoth-he) I will shew you none / go sue me / go sue me.
Then sayd one of the merchants / doe you thus vse vs for
asking our due ? Wee would you should know / we are no
suche vile persons. Done Iohn of London (hearing their
answere) cried out / saying : Hence away / Citizens ? Dumbe Iohn
nay you are raskcals / you are worse then wicked of Londons
blessing
mammon (so lifting vp both his hands / and flinging them
downe againe / said) You are theeues / you are Coseners : take
that for a bishops blessing / and so get you hence. But when
they would haue aunswered / his men thrust them out of the
dores. But shortly after / he perceiued they went about to
bring the matter to farther tryial : he sent a messenger vnto
them confessing the debt / but they cannot get their money to
this day. What reason is it they should haue their mony ?

hath he not bestowed his liberallitie alreadie on them? Can they not be satisfied with the blessing of this braue bounsing priest? But brethren bishops / I pray you tell me? hath not your brother London / a notable brazen face to vse these men so for their owne? I told you / Martin will be proued no lyar / in that he saith that Bb. are cogging and cosening knaues. This priest went to buffets with his sonne in law / for a bloodie nose / well fare all good tokens. The last lent there came a commaundement from his grace into Paules Churchyard / that no Byble should be bounde without the Apocripha. Monstrous and vngodly wretches / that to maintaine their owne outragious proceedings / thus mingle heauen and earth together / and woulde make the spirite of God / to be the author of prophane bookes. I am hardly drawn to a merie vaine from such waightie matters.

But you see my worshipfull priestes of this crue to whom I write / what a perilous fellow M. Marprelate is: he vnderstands of all your knauerie / and it may be he keepes a register of of them : vnlesse you amend / they shall al come into the light one day. And you brethren bishops / take this warning from me. If you doe not leaue your persecuting of godly christians and good subiectes / that seeke to liue vprightly in the feare of God / and the obedience of her Maiestie / all your dealing shalbe made knowen vnto the world. And ise be sure to make you an example to all posterities. You see I haue taken some paynes with you alreadie / and I will owe you a better turne / and pay it you with aduauntage / at the least thirteene to the dozen / vnles you obserue these conditions of peace which I drawe betweene me and you. For I assure you I make not your doings known ior anie mallice that I beare vnto you / but the hurt that you doe vnto Gods Churche / leaue you your wickednesse / and ile leaue the reuealing of your knaueries.

☞ **Conditions of Peace to be inuiolablie kept for euer / betweene the reuerend and worthy master Martin Marprelate gentleman on the one partie / and the reuerend fathers his brethren / the Lord bishops of this lande.**

1 *IN primis,* the said Lord Bb. must promise and obserue / without fraud or collusion / and that as much as in them lyeth / they labor to promote the preaching of the worde in euery part of this land.

2 That hereafter they admitt none vnto the ministerie / but such as shalbe knowen / both for their godlinesse and learning / to be fit for the ministerie / and not these neyther without cure / vnlesse they be Colledge ministers of eyther of the Vniuersities / and in no case they suffer any to be nonresidents: and that they suffer M. Cartwrightes answere to the Rhemish Testament to be published.

3 That neyther they nor their seruants / vz. their Archdeacons / Chancellors / nor any other of the high commission / which serue their vile affections / vrge any to subscribe contrary to the statute 13. Eliza. and that they suspend or silence none / but such / as either for their false doctrine / or euill life / shall shew themselues / to be vnworthy the places of ministers: so that none be suspended or silenced / eyther for speaking (when their text giueth them occasion) against the corruptions of the Church / for refusing to weare the surplice / cap / tippet / &c / or omitting the corruptions of the booke of common prayers / as churching of women / the crosse in baptisme / the ring in marriage / &c.

4 That none be molested by them or any their aforesaid seruants / for this my booke / for not kneeling at the communion / or for resorting on the Saboth (if they haue not preachers of their owne) to heare the word preached / and to receiue the Sacraments.

5 Lastly / that neuer hereafter they profane excommunication as they haue done / by excommunicating alone in their chambers / and that for trifles: yea before mens causes be heard. That they neuer forbid publike fasts / molest either preacher / or hearer / for being present at such assemblies. Briefly / that they neuer slander the cause of reformation / or the furtherers thereof / in terming the cause by the name of Anabaptisterie / schisme / &c. and the men puritans / and enemies to the state.

These be the conditions / which you brethren bishops / shalbe bound to keepe inuiolably on your behalfe. And I your brother Martin on the other side / do faithfully promise vpon the performaunce of the premisses by you / neuer to make any more of your knauery knowne vnto the worlde. And howbeit that I haue before threatened my brother Bridges / in the cause of his superior priest / and your Antichristian callings : notwithstanding / I will write no more of your dealings / vnles you violate the former conditions. The conditions you see / are so reasonable / I might binde you to giue ouer your places which are Antichristian : but I doe not / lest men shoulde thinke me to quarrell / and seeke occasions for the nonce to fall out with my brethren. Therefore I require no more but such things as all the worlde will thinke you vnworthy to liue / if you grant them not. And this I doe the rather / because you should not / according to your olde fashion / say yat my worship doth for mallice lay open your infirmities : nay I haue published not one of your secret falts / what you haue not blushed to commit in the face of the sun / and in the iust[i]fiing wherof you yet stand / these things onely haue I published. The best seruants of God I know / haue their infirmities. But none of them will stand in the maintenance of their corruptions as you do / and that to the dishonour of God and the ruine of his Church. You must either amend / or shortly you will bring our church to ruine : therfore it is time that your dealings were better looked vnto

You will go about I know / to proue my booke to be a libell / but I haue preuented you of yat aduantage in lawe / both in bringing in nothing but matters of fact / whiche may easily be prooued / if you dare denie them : and also in setting my name to my booke. Well I offer you peace vpon the former conditions / if you will keepe them / but if you violate them either in whole or in part (for why should you breake anye one of them) then your learned brother Martin doth proclaime open war against you / and entendeth to worke your woe 2. maner of wayes as followeth. First I will watch you

at euery halfe turne / and whatsoeuer you do amisse / I will
presently publish it : you shall not call one honest man before
you / but I will get his examination (and you thinke I shall
knowe nothing of the oppression of your tenants by your
briberie / &c.) and publish it / if you deal not according to the
former conditions. To this purpose I wil place a yong Martin
in euerie diocesse / which may take notice of your practizes.
Do you think that you shalbe suffred any longer / to break the
law of God / and to tyrannize ouer his people her Maiesties
subiectes / and no man tell you of it ? No I warrant you.
And rather then I will be disappointed of my purpose / I will
place a Martin in euerie parish. In part of Suffolk and Essex /
I thinke I were best to haue 2. in a parishe. I hope in time
they shalbe as worthie Martins as their father is / euery one
of them able to mar a prelate. Marke what wil be the issue
of these things / if you still keep your olde byas. I know you
would not haue your dealings so knowne vnto the worlde / as
I and my sonnes will blase them. Secondly / al the books
that I haue in store already of your doings / shalbe published
vpon the breache of the former couenants or any of them.
Here I know some will demand what these bookes are / because
saith one / I warrant you / there will be old sport / I hope olde
father Palinod D. Perne / shall be in there by the weekes.
Why my masters of the cleargie / did you neuer heare of my
books in deed ? Foe / then you neuer heard of good sport in
your life. The catalogue of their names / and the arguments
of some are as followeth. As for my booke named Mine Epitom[e]
Epistomastix, I make no mention thereof at this is readie.
time. First my *Paradoxes*, 2. my *Dialogues*, 3. my *Miscelanea*,
4. my *Variæ leiciones*, 5. *Martins dreame*, 6. *Of the liues and
doings of English popes*, 7. my *Itinerarium, or visitations*, 8. my
Lambathismes. In my *Paradoxes* shalbe handled som points /
which the common sort haue not greatly considered of : as 1
That our prelats / if they professed popery / could not do so
much hurt vnto Gods Church as now they do. 2 That the
Diuell is not better practized in bowling and swering then
Iohn of London is / with other like points. What shalbe
handled in my 2. 3. 4. 5. and 6. bookes / you shall know when
you read them.
    Mine *It[in]erarium* shalbe a booke of no great profit / eyther
to the Church or commonwealth : and yet had neede to be in

follio / or else iudge you by this that followeth. I meane to make a suruey into all the diocesse in this land / that I may keepe a visitation among my cleargie men. I would wish them to keepe good rule / and to amend their manners against I come. For I shall paint them in their coulers / if I finde any thing amisse : In this booke I wil note all their memorable pranckes. As for example / if I finde anye priest to haue done as Sir Gefferie Iones of Warwicke shire did / that must be set downe in my visitations / and I thinke I had need to haue many Scribes / and many reames of paper for this purpose. The said sir Iefferie Iones / committed a part verie well beseeming his priesthood / which was after this maner. Sir Ieffry once in an alehouse (I doe desire the reader to beare with me / though according to M. Bridges his fashion / I write false Englishe in this sentence) whereunto he resorted for his morning draught / either because his hostesse woulde haue him pay the olde score before he should run any further / or the new / or els because the gamesters his companions wan all his monie at trey trip : tooke such vnkindenes at the alehouse / that he sware he would neuer goe againe into it. Although this rash vow of the good priest / was made to the great losse of the alewife / ˙ who by means of sir Iefferie was woont to haue good vtterance for her ale : yet I think the tap had great quietnes and ease therby / which coulde not be quiet so much as an houre in the day / as long as Sir Iefferie resorted vnto the house / how sweete it was / poore sir Iones felt the discommoditie of his rashe vowe. Then alas / he was in a woe case / as you know : for his stomacke could not be at all strengthened with the drink he got abroad. But better were a man not to feele his discommoditie / then not to be able to redresse the same. Therefore at length sir Iefferie bethought him of a feat whereby he might both visit the alestond / and also keepe his othe. And so he hired a man to carie him vpon his backe to the alehouse / by this meanes he did not goe / but was caried thither / wherevnto he made a vow neuer to go. I doubt not in my visitation / but to get a hundreth of these stratagemes / especially if I trauell neere where any of the vickers of hell are. As in Surrie / Northampton / and Oxforde shires. And I would wish the Purcivants and the Stacioners / with the Woolfe their beadle / not to be so redy:

to molest honest men. And Stacioners / I would wish you
not to be so francke with your bribes / as you were to Thomas
Draper / I can tell you his grace had need to prouide a bag
ful of Items for you / if you be be so liberal. Were you so
foolish (or so malicious against Walde-graue) to giue that
knaue Draper fiue pounds to betray him into your wretched
hands : he brought you to Kingstone vpon Thames / with
Purcivants to take him / where he should be a printing books
in a Tinkars house. (your selues being disguised so / that
Walde-graue might not know you / for of Citizens you were
becom[e] ruffians) There you were to seek that could not be
found / and many such iournies may you make. But when
you came to London / you laid Thomas Draper in the
Counter for cosenage. O well bowlde / when Iohn of London
throwes his bowle / he will runne after it / and crie rub /
rub / rub / and say the diuill go with thee. But what
thinke you shalbe handled in my *Lambathismes*? Truely
this / I will there make a comparison of Iohn Whitgifts
Canterburines / with Iohn Bridges his Lambathismes. To
speake in plaine English / I will there set downe the flowers
of errors / popishe and others / wherewith those two worthie
men haue stuffed the bookes which they haue written / against
the cause of reformation / in the defence of the gouernment
of Bb. I haue in this book as you shal see / gathered some
flowers out of Iohn of Londons booke / but my Lambathismes
shalbe done otherwise I trow.

And now if it may please you of the Confocationhouse / to
here of any of the former books / then break the league
which I offer to make with you / but if you woulde haue my
friendship / as I seeke yours / then let me see that you
persecute no more / and especially / that you trouble none
for this booke of mine. For this must be an especiall article
of our agreement / as you know. And Deane Iohn / for your
part / you must plaie the fool no more in the pulpit : we will
end this matter with a prettie storie / of a certaine mischance
that befell a B. corner cap / as followeth. Olde doctor
Turner (I meane not D. Perne the old turner) had a dog full
of good quallities. D. Turner hauing inuited a B. to his
table / in dinner while called his dog / and told him that the
B. did sweat (you must think he labored hard ouer his
trencher) The dogg flies at the B. and tooke of[f] his corner

capp (he thought belike it had bene a cheese cake) and so away goes the dog with it to his master. Truely my masters of the cleargie / I woulde neuer weare corner cap againe / seeing dogs runne away with them : and here endeth the storie.

May it please you that are of this house / to tell me the cause / when you haue leysure / why so many opinions and errors are risen in our Church / concerning the ministery / and the ioyning with preaching and vnpreaching ministers. To tell you my opinion in your eare / I thinke it to be want of preaching / and I thinke your worships to haue bene the cause of all this stir. Some puritans holde readers for no ministers / som[e] hold you our worthy Bb. for little better then faire parchment readers / and say that you haue no learning. Now whether readers be ministers or no / and whether our bishops be learned or no / I woulde wish you brethren bishops / and you brethren· puritans / to make no great controuersie / but rather labor that all euil ministers may be turned out of the Church / and so I hope there shoulde be a speedie ende of all those questions betweene you. For then I doubt not / but that Lord bishops whereat the puritans so repine / shoulde be in a faire reckoning within short space / euen the next to the dore saue the dog : and I see that you bishopps are well towardes this promotion alreadie. And truely / though the puritans should neuer so much repine at the matter / yet I tell you true / I am glad that you are so esteemed among men. And for mine owne part / I think my masters / that manie of you our Lord Bb. and cleargie men / are men verie notorious for their learning and preaching. And hereof vnder Benedicite betweene you and me / (the puritanes may stand aside nowe) I will bring you some instances. First his grace and my L. of Winchester haue bene verie notable clarkes / euer since M. doctor Sparke set them at a *non plus* (some of their honors being present) in the conference betweene him and M. Trauers on the puritans side / and the two Archbishops and the B. of Winchester on the other side. D. Sparks argument was drawn from the corruption of the translation of the 28. verse of the 105. Psalme / in the booke of Common Prayer / and the contrarietie of the translations allowed by the Bb. themselues. For in the book of Common Prayer you shal read thus :

And they were not obedient vnto his word (which is a plain
corruption of the text) in other priuiledged English translations
it is / And they were not disobedient vnto his word / which
is according to the veritie of the originall. By the way ere
I go any further / I would know with what conscience / either
my brother Cant. or any els of our Bb. can vrge men to
allow such palpable corruptions by subscribing vnto thinges
meere contrarie to the word. Here also I would shew by
the way / and I woulde haue al my sonnes to note / that
their vncle Canterburies drift in vrging subscription / is not
the vnity of the church (as he would pretende) but the
maintenance of his owne pride and corruption / which should
soon come to ye ground / if the worde had free passage :
and therefore he prooueth the same / by stopping the mouthes
of ye sincere preachers thereof. For if the vnitie of the
Church had bene his end / why hath not he amended this
fault in all the books that haue bene printed since that time /
which now is not so little as 3. yeares / in which time / many
thousand of books of Common praier haue bin printed. If
he had other busines in hand then the amending of the
booke of Common prayer ? why had he not / nay why doth
he not leaue vrging of subscription vntill that be amended ?
Can he and his hirelings haue time to imprison and depriue
men / because they will not sinne / by approuing lyes vpon
the holy ghost (which thinges they cannot / nor could not
chuse but committ / whosoeuer will or haue subscribed vnto
the booke and Articles) And can he haue no time in 3. or 4.
yeares to correct most grose and vngodly faultes in the print /
whereof the putting out of one syllable / euen three letters
(dis) would haue amended this place. But it lieth not in his
grace to amende the corruptions of the booke. Belike it
lieth in him to doe nothing but sinne / and to compell men
against their consciences to sinne / or else to bring extreme -
miserie vpon them. If it laye not in him / yet he might haue
acquainted the Parliament (for there was a Parliament since
the time he knew this fault) with the corruptions of the
booke. And I will come neerer home to him then so / in the
Article concerning the gouernment whereunto men are vrged
to subscribe. You must (say the Articles) protest that there
is nothing in the ministery of the Church of England / that is
not according to ye word / or to such like effect they speake.

I say that I cannot subscribe vnto this article / because
contrary to the expresse commandement of our sauiour Christ /
and the examples of his Apostles / there be Lords in yat
ministerie / or such as wold be accounted ministers / wil also
be called and accounted Lords / and bear ciuill offices / the
words of Christ are those. The kinges of the Gentil[e]s raigne
ouer them / and they that beare rule ouer them / are called
gracious Lords / but you shall not be so / Luk[e]. 22. 25. 26. I
saye that out of this place / it is manifest / that it is vtterly
vnlawfull for a minister to be a Lord : that is / for any L. B. to
be in the ministerie : and therefore I cannot subscribe vnto
that Article which would haue me iustifie this to be lawfull.
Nowe I will cease this point / because I doubt not but the
Articles of subscription / wilbe shortly so made out of fashion /
that the Bb. will be ashamed of them themselues : and if no
other will take them in hande / ile turne one of mine owne
breede vnto them / eyther Martin senior / or some of his
brethren.

To go forward / his Lordship of Winchester is a great
Clarke / for he hath translated his Dictionarie / called Co[o]pers
Dictionarie / verbatim out of Robert Stephanus his Thesaurus /
and ilfauored to[o] they say. But what do I speake of our
bishops learning / as long as bishop Ouerton / bishopp Bickley /
bishop Middleton / the Deane of Westminster / doctor Cole /
D. Bell / with many others / are liuing / I doubt me whether
all the famous dunses be dead. And if you woulde haue an
ilsample of an excellent pulpit man in deede / go no further
then the B. of Glocester now liuing : And in him you shall
finde a plaine instance of such a one as I meane. On a time
he preaching at Worcester before he was B. vpon Sir Iohns
day : as he trauersed his matter / and discoursed vpon many
points / he came at the length vnto the very pithe of his whol[e]
sermon / contained in the distinction of the name of Iohn /
which he then shewing all his learning at once / full learnedly
handled after this manner. Iohn / Iohn / the grace of God /
the grace of God / the grace of God : gracious Iohn / not
graceles Iohn / but gracious Iohn. Iohn / holy Iohn / holy Iohn /
not Iohn ful of holes / but holy Iohn If he shewed not himselfe
learned in this sermond / then hath he bene a duns all his
life. In the same sermon / two seuerall Iohns / the father
and the sonne / that had beene both recusants / being brought

publikely to confesse their faults / this worthy doctor / by reason that the yong man hauing bene poysoned beyond the seas with popery / was more obstinate then his father / and by all likelihood / he was ye cause of his fathers peruersnesse : with a vehement exclamation / able to pearce a cobweb / called on the father aloud in this patheticall and perswading sort. Old Iohn / olde Iohne / be not led away by the Syren sounds / and intisements of yong Iohn / if yong Iohn will go to the diuell / the diuell go with him. The puritans it may be / will here obiect / that this worthy man was endued with these famous gifts before he was B. whereas since that time / say they / he is not able to say bo to a goose. You wey this man belike my masters / according to the rest of our Bb. But I assure you it is not so with him. For the last Lent in a sermon he made in Glocester towne / he shewed him selfe to be the man that he was before. For he did in open pulpit confirme the trueth of his text to be authenticall / being the prophesie of Isaiah / out of the book of Common prayer / which otherwise would (it is to be feared) haue proued Apocrypha. His text was / a childe is borne vnto vs / which after he sweetly repeated very often as before / to the great destruction and admiration of the hearers / saying : A child is borne / a child is borne / a child is borne vnto us this (sayth he) is proued you know / where in that worthy verse of the booke of Common prayer. Thy honorable true and onely sonne. Afterward / repeating the same words againe : A childe is borne vnto vs / a chi[l]de is borne vnto vs : here sayth hee / I might take occasion to commende that worthy verse in our Latenie / where this is made very manifest / that ye prophet here speaketh. By thy Natiuitie and circumcision. What should I prosecute the condemnation of this man / as though other our Bb. and pulpit men haue not as commendable gifts as he.

And once againe to you brother Bridges / you haue set downe a flanting reason / in the 75. page of your book / against the continuance of the gouernment which the Puritans labor for / and I finde the same syllogisme concluded in no mood : therefore what if I was ashamed to put it downe ? But seeing it is your will / to laye on the puritans with it as it is / put your corner cap a litle nere a toe [at one] side / that we may see your partie coullered beard / and with what a manly countenance/you giue your brethren this scouring. And I hope this will please you/my cleargie masters/as well as if I tolde you how our brother Bridges plaid my L. of Winchesters foole/in sir Maries pulpit in Cambridg[e]/but no word of that : now to my reason.

Some kinde of ministerie ordained by the Lorde/was temporarie (saith he) as for example / the Mosaicall priesthood / and the ministerie of Apostles / prophets / &c. But the ministerie of pastors/doctors/elders and deacons / was ordayned by the Lord : Therefore it was temporarie.

Alacke / alacke deane Iohn / what haue you done now? The puritanes will be O the bones of you too badd/for this kinde of arguing/and they wil reason after this sort.

1 Some man in the land (say they) weareth a wooden dagger and a coxcombe / as for example / his grace of Canterburies foole/doctor Pernes cosen and yours : you presbyter Iohn Catercap/are some man in the land : Therefore by this reason / you weare a woodden dagger and a coxcombe.

2 Some presbyter prieste or elder in the English ministerie/is called the vicker of hell. As for example one about Oxford/another neere Northampton/and the parson of Micklaim in Surrie : But the dean of Sarum Iohn Catercap/ is some priest in the Englishe ministerie : Ergo he is the vicker of hell.

3 Some presbyter priest or elder / preaching at Pauls crosse 1587. tould a tale of a leadden shoinghorne/and spake of Catekissing : and preaching at the Court on another time/thrust his hand into his pocket/and drew out a piece of sarsnet/saying/behold a relique of Maries smocke : and thrusting his hand into the other pocket/drew out either a linnen or a wollen rag/saying/behold a relique of Iosephs breeches. But quoth he/there is no reason why Maries smocke shoulde be of sarsnet/seeing Iosephs breeches were not of silke. This pri[e]st being lately demanded whether he should be bishop of Eli/answered that he had now no great hope to B. of Eli : and therefore quoth he/I may say well inough/Eli/Eli/Lammasabacthani. Eli/Eli/why hast thou forsaken me. Alluding very blasphemously vnto the words which our Sauioure Christe spake/in his greatest agonie vpon the crosse. The same priest calling before him one M.

Benison a preacher / and would haue vrged him to take his
othe / to answere to such articles as he would propounde against
him / who answered saying / brother bishop / I wil not sweare /
except I know to what ? with that the priest fell sicke of the
splene / and began to sweare by his fayth : quoth Benison / a
Bishop should preach fayth / and not not sweare by it. This
priest being in his malancholicke mood / sent him to the
Clincke / where he lay till her Maiestie was made priuie of
his tyrannie / and then released to the priests wo[e]. As for
example / the B. of London did al those things and more to :
For lying at his house at Haddam in Essex / vpon the
Sabboth day (wanting his bowling mates) tooke his seruantes
and went a heymaking / the godly ministers round about
being exercised (though against his commandement) in
fasting and prayer : But you Iohn Catercap / are some
presbyter priest or Elder : Therefore you prophaned the
word and ministerie in this sort.

4 Some presbyter priest or elder in the land / is accused
(and euen now the matter is in triall before his grace and
his brethren) to haue two wiues / and to marie his brother
vnto a woman vpon her death bedd / shee being past
recouerie. As for example / the B. of sir Dauies in wales /
is this priest as they saye : But you presbyter Iohn / are
some priest : Therefore you haue committed all these
vnnaturall parts.

5 Some priest preaching at the funeralls of one who died /
not onely being condemned by the lawe of God and of the
land / for attempting matters against her Maiesties person
and the state / but also dyed an obstinate and professed
papist / and without anye repentance for her enterprises
against her Maiestie and the state : prayed that his soule
and the soules of all the rest there present / might be with
the soule of the vnrepentant papist departed. As for
example / the B. of Lincolne did this at Peterborough /
August. 2. 1587. But you are some priest : Ergo you made
such a prayer.

6 Some priest in ye land lately made / or verie shortly
meaneth to make / as they say / an olde acquaintance of
his owne / Richard Patrick / clothier of Worcester / of the
reading ministery. As for example / his grace of Canter. is
this priest : But you brother Sarum are som priest as wel

as he : Ergo you haue thrust a bankerout clothier in the
ministerie.

7 Some priest hauing giuen a man (whose wife had
plaid the harlot) leaue to marie another / desiring the
man long after he had bene maried to another woman / to
shewe him his letters of diuorcement / with promise to deliuer
them againe : But hauing receiued them / they are retained
of him most iniuriously vnto this day / and he troubleth the
man for hauing two wiues : as for example / the B. of sir
Asse is this priest : But you dean Catercap are som priest
Ergo you do men such open iniurie.

8 Some men that breake the lawe of God are traytors to her
Maiestie / as for example / the Iesuites.   But all our bishops
are some men that breake the lawe of God / because they
continue in vnlawful callings : Ergo by your reason they are
traitors to her maiestie / but I deny your argument / for there
may be manie breaches of the law of God / whereof they may
be guiltie / and yet no traytors.

9 Some men that will not haue their Lordships / and their
callings examined by the worde / are limbs of Antichrist / as
for example / the Pope and his Cardinals : But our L. bishops
are some men which will not haue their lordships and their
callings tried by the word :   Therfore they are limbs of
Antichrist.

10 Some men would play the turncoats / with the B. of
Glocester / D. Renold / D. Perne (I wil let D. Goodman
Abbot of West. alone now) But all the L. bishops / and you
brother catercap are some men : Ergo you would becom
papists againe.

11 Some men dare not dispute with their aduersaries / lest
their vngodly callings shoulde be ouerthrowen / and they
compelled to walke more orderly : But our Bb. are some men :
Ergo they dare not dispute lest their vngodly callings and
places shoulde be ouerthrowen.

12 Som men are theeues and soul murtherers before God /
as for example / all nonresidents : Euerie L. bishop is a
nonresident : Ergo he is a thiefe and a soule murtherer
before God.

13 Some men are become Apostates from their ministerie /
sinners against their owne consciences / persecuters of their
brethren / sacriligious Church robbers / withstanders of the

known trueth / for their owne filthie lukers sake / and are
afraid lest the gospel and the holy discipline thereof should
be receiued in euerie place: But our Bb. are some men:
Therfore (by your reson M. doctor) they are become
Apostaes from their ministerie / sinners against their owne
consciences / persecutors of their brethren / sacriligious Church
robbers / and withstanders of the knowen trueth / &c.

14 Som priest is a pope / as for example / that priest
which is bishop of Rome is a Pope: But his grace of Cant.
is some priest: Therefore M. Bridges / by your maner of
reasoning / he is a Pope.

You may see what harme you haue done by dealing so
loosely. I knowe not what I shall say to these puritans
reasons? They must needs be good / if yours be sound.
Admit their syllogisms offended in form as yours doth: yet
the common people / and especially dame Lawson / and the
gentlewoman / whose man demanded of her / when she sat at
the B. of Londons fire: why mistris wil you sit by Caiphas
his fire? will finde an vnhappy trueth in many of these
conclusions / when as yours is most false. And many of
their propositions are tried truths / hauing many eye and
eare witnesses liuing.

Men when commonly they dedicate bookes vnto any / enter
into commendations of those vnto whom they write. But I
care not an I owe you my cleargie masters a commendations /
and pay you when you better deserue it. In stead thereof /
I will giue you some good counsel and aduice / which if you
followe / I assure you it will be the better for you.

First I would aduise you as before I haue said / to set at
libertie all the preachers that you haue restrained from
preaching: otherwise it shalbe the worse for you / my reason
is this. The people are altogether discontented for want of
teachers. Some of them alreadie runne into corners / and
more are like / because you keepe the meanes of knowledge
from them. Running into corners will breed Anabaptistrie /
Anabaptistrie will allienate the heartes of the subiects from
their lawfull gouernour. And you are the cause hereof. And
wil not her Maiestie then think you / require the hearts of
her subiectes at your handes / when she shal vnderstand that
they are alienated (as God forbid they should) from her by
your means? yes I warrant you. And if they should put vp

a supplication vnto her highnesse / that their preachers might be restored vnto them / I doubt not but they should be heard. I can tell you she tendreth the estate of her people / and will not discourage their hearts / in casting of[f] their suits / to maynetaine your pride and couetousnesse : you were then better to set the preachers at libertie / then to suffer your cruelty and euill dealing to be made known vnto her. For so they shall be sure I doubt not to preuaile in their suit / and you to go by the worse. And try if her Maiestie be not shortly mooued in this suit. To it my masters roundly / you that meane to deale herein / and on my life you set the prelats in such a quandare / as they shal not know wher to stand. Now M. Prelates I will giue you some more counsell / follow it. Repent cleargie men / and especially bishopps / preach fayth Bb. and sweare no more by it / giue ouer your Lordly callings : reform your families and your children : They are the patterne of loosenesse / withstand not the knowen trueth no longer : you haue seduced her Maiestie and hir people. Praye her Maiestie to forgiue you / and the Lord first to put away your sinnes. Your gouerment is Antichristian / deceiue the Lord no longer therby : You wil grow from euil to worse vnlesse betimes you return. You are now worse then you were 29. yeeres ago : write no more against the cause of reformation : Your vngodlinesse is made more manifest by your writings : And because you cannot answer what hath bene written against you / yeeld vnto the trueth. If you should write / deale syllogistically : For you shame your selues / when you vse any continued speach / because your stile is so rude and barbarous. Raile no more in the pulpitt against good men / you do more hurt to your selues / and your owne desperat cause / in one of your rayling sermons / then you could in speaking for reformation. For euerie man that hath any light of religion in him will examine your groundes / which being found ridiculous (as they are) will be decided / and your cause made odious. Abuse not the high commission as you do / against the best subiects. The commission it selfe was ordained for very good purposes / but it is most horriblie abused by you / and turned cleane contrarie to the ende wherefore it was ordayned. Helpe the poore people to the meanes of their saluation / that perish in their ignorance:

make restitution vnto your tenants / and such as from whome
you haue wrongfully extorted any thing : Vsurpe no longer /
the authoritie of making of ministers and excommunication :
Let poore men be no more molested in your vngodly courts :
Studie more then you doe / and preache oftener : Fauor
nonresidents and papists no longer : labor to clense ye
ministery of the swarms of ignorant guides / wherewith it
hath bin defiled : Make conscience of breaking the Sabboth /
by bowling and tabling : Be ringleaders of prophanenes no
longer vnto the people : Take no more bribes : Leaue your
Symonie : Fauor learning more then you doe / and especially
godly learning : Stretch your credit if you haue any / to the
furtherance of the gospell : You haue ioyned the prophanation
of the magistracie / to the corruption of the ministerie :
Leaue this sinne. All in a word / become good christians /
and so you shall become good subiects / and leaue your
tyrannie. And I would aduise you / let me here no more of
your euill dealing.

   Giuen at my Castle between two wales / neither foure
dayes from penilesse benche / nor yet at the West ende of
Shrofftide : but the foureteenth yeare at the least / of the
age of Charing crosse / within a yeare of Midsom-
mer / betweene twelue and twelue of the clocke.

Anno pontificatus vestri Quinto, and
I hope *vltimo* of all Englishe Popes.

By your learned and worthie brother:
Martin Marprelate.

www.ingramcontent.com/pod-product-compliance
Lightning Source LLC
Chambersburg PA
CBHW030854260626
47169CB00008B/2533

* 9 7 8 3 3 3 7 7 2 8 9 1 5 *